NOTHING VENTURED, NOTHING GAINED

NOTHING VENTURED, NOTHING GAINED

Rewiring the DNA in Banking

BY

ALEX MANSON
Standard Chartered Ventures, Singapore

United Kingdom – North America – Japan
India – Malaysia – China

Emerald Publishing Limited
Emerald Publishing, Floor 5, Northspring, 21-23 Wellington Street, Leeds LS1 4DL.

First edition 2025

Copyright © 2025 SCV Master Holding Company Pte Ltd, Singapore.
Published under exclusive licence by Emerald Publishing limited.

Reprints and permissions service
Contact: www.copyright.com

No part of this book may be reproduced, stored in a retrieval system, transmitted in any form or by any means electronic, mechanical, photocopying, recording or otherwise without either the prior written permission of the publisher or a licence permitting restricted copying issued in the UK by The Copyright Licensing Agency and in the USA by The Copyright Clearance Center. Any opinions expressed in the chapters are those of the authors. Whilst Emerald makes every effort to ensure the quality and accuracy of its content, Emerald makes no representation implied or otherwise, as to the chapters' suitability and application and disclaims any warranties, express or implied, to their use.

British Library Cataloguing in Publication Data
A catalogue record for this book is available from the British Library

ISBN: 978-1-83708-309-1 (Print)
ISBN: 978-1-83708-306-0 (Online)
ISBN: 978-1-83708-308-4 (Epub)

INVESTOR IN PEOPLE

CONTENTS

Standard Chartered Book Disclaimer   vii

Foreword   ix

Preface   xiii

1 The Genesis of SC Ventures   1

2 Catalysing Internal Innovation   9

3 CardsPal: Credit Card Rewards Made Easy   15

4 The eXellerator: Welcoming Startups with Empathy   23

5 The eXellerator: Old Meets New   31

6 TASConnect: The Operating System of Trade   39

7 The eXellerator: New Meets Old   45

8 Building the SC Ventures FinTech Bridge   51

9 Corporate Venture Capital Investment: Too Close or Too Far — Rarely Just Right   57

10 The Birth of Jarvis   63

11 Creating Optionality for Banking through New Ventures   67

12 Venture Building: Designing a Clear Path for Ideas   81

13 The Road Ahead: Corporate Venturing *Quo Vadis?*   87

14 SOLV: A B2B E-Commerce Marketplace for Small Businesses   93

15 Audax: Transforming Banking Technology from Legacy to Limitless   101

16	Rewiring the DNA through Experimentation	109
17	Cultural Prerogatives: Diverse and Flat	125
18	The Biggest Enabler: Culture	135
19	Autumn	143
20	The Role of Technology in SC Ventures	151
21	Mox: A New, Virtual Bank	155
22	Control Prerogatives: Getting the Governance Right	165
23	Zodia: Rethinking the Role of Banks in the Crypto Revolution	171
24	Compliance: The Agile Compliance Officer	177
25	Legal: The T-Shaped Counsel	181
26	Finance: Cash is King	187
27	Afterword: Brace Yourself for More Change	193

References   *197*

STANDARD CHARTERED
BOOK DISCLAIMER

This publication is intended for general informational purposes only and may contain contributions from third-party contributors.

All views expressed are those of the individual and do not reflect the views of Standard Chartered or the Standard Chartered Group.

This publication does not constitute an offer, recommendation or solicitation to enter into any transaction or financial advice. It has not been prepared for any particular person or class of persons and is not to be taken in substitution for the exercise of judgment by the reader, who should obtain independent advice.

FOREWORD

I joined Standard Chartered Bank in hope that I could build on our rich history, unique footprint, trusted brand, diversity of people and above all our compelling tagline: Here for Good. As a CEO, I was excited by the challenge of transforming this great bank into a future-proof institution.

But first we needed to address some of the challenges the bank was facing at the time. In 2015 we embarked on a multi-year strategy: secure the foundations, become lean and focused, and invest and innovate. Having made significant progress against the first two pillars, in 2018 we set up SC Ventures to accelerate our transformation as an innovative driver of growth. A lot of good work was going on within the business units, but we needed a catalyst and a platform to drive culture change across the bank. We set up SC Ventures differently from most banks or corporates – it combined an innovation lab, an investment fund and venture building, all under one discrete business unit.

There was some resistance from my management team – not so much about the 'why we need to do this' but about 'how we are going about it'. The why was clear: it is existential for the banking sector to evolve, build trust with clients, and embrace new technology. As to the 'how', traditional wisdom says that the innovation mandate should rest within the business units. Our approach was different though: we believed that if we aspire to change the bank, we should be prepared to disrupt our own business. Hence SC Ventures was set up as an integral part of the bank, which every employee can leverage as a platform, but also had the ability to be completely distinct and a separate incubator for great ideas.

I was also challenged as to why we, Standard Chartered, are well positioned to do this and what advantages we bring to the table? First, we are a regulated institution, meaning we have experience with what it takes to bring bank grade data governance and security to our applications. Second, we are good partners. The bank is large enough to be meaningful in the markets in which we operate, yet small enough to partner with others.

SC Ventures started as an experiment. In a short period of time, it has had significant impact on a number of areas, beyond financials. Here are my top three:

First and foremost, it is our clients. We wanted to be disruptive with a purpose. We were prepared to experiment with business models and disrupt ourselves (and other incumbents) to address unmet customer needs in our markets, which in many cases we see and hear first-hand from our clients. Early feedback from our clients has been very encouraging: not only do they have better user experience thanks to our digital transformation, but they also get access to newer, innovative offerings from our digital banks, banking as a service (BaaS) or small and medium-sized enterprise (SME) platforms. During one of our 'Investor Days', I promised the audience that we will continue to be 'your father's bank', but we are much more likely in the future to be your daughter's bank or your granddaughter's bank. Because what we are building is future fit.

Second is culture and mindset. Some of the takeaways from this book apply to any leader in any business. In particular, the concept of unlearning certain reflexes, and training new muscles so you can leap towards transformation. In large organisations, people tend to 'wear a well-worn hat' or play a narrowly defined role. Yet, one of the most important factors for success may be our willingness to step outside of such narrow roles, without losing our core expertise and accountability. By building an external mindset and at the same time disrupting from within, SC Ventures has indeed been a catalyst for the bank. On one hand, thousands of 'Intrapreneurs' came forward with ideas to build new products or even businesses. On the other hand, business units within the bank pursued their own innovation efforts, leveraging what they learned from SC Ventures. The result is that we all became even more client centric.

Foreword

Finally, the impact on strategy and our 'bold stands'. SC Ventures challenged the strategy and entered businesses which many thought would be off-strategy or not something in which we could compete. We were one of the first banks to embrace the new digital assets environment, beginning with cryptocurrency. Through our BaaS model, we approached mass retail in a different way. We were challenged to build a scalable business model for SMEs in some of our markets, which prompted us to take a digital platform approach to this segment. Beyond strategy, SC Ventures is also core to the delivery of our stands – Accelerating Zero, Lifting Participation and Resetting Globalisation.

To be clear, we are not declaring success yet. There are many challenges to overcome as SC Ventures enters the next phase of its growth story. But we do know that what we have embarked on, started is fundamental to the transformation of the bank and banking. Many corporates and other financial institutions have asked us about the lessons learnt and how we scaled this experiment, and I hope the readers will benefit from the diversity of stories we have in this book. While SC Ventures is integral to our transformation and innovation agenda, its ambition is much bigger – to rewire the DNA in banking.

Bill Winters
CEO, Standard Chartered Bank

PREFACE

It was a cold, wet London day when I had my first meeting with Standard Chartered Bank, upon joining in 2012. Entering their headquarters seemed like entering a different world. The lobby was adorned with Asian and African artefacts, my pass was handed to me with both hands – the Asian way – and the receptionist ushered me to a meeting room, while telling stories about the Bank.

All meeting rooms in the building exhibit paintings that represent 'faces of the footprint'. In this particular room, it was smiling children from South Asia, but you could equally be met by portraits of people from anywhere in Asia, Africa or the Middle East. It is a reminder of the human impact of the Bank's presence (170 years in some of these markets).

At the time of joining Standard Chartered Bank, I was in the process of leaving my previous employer and heading to another great financial institution. Yet, the Bank's brand promise, 'Here for Good' was too intriguing to resist. It evoked an emotional attachment between the Bank, its footprint markets, and its clients.

This was set in a backdrop of when modern capitalism was beginning to take stakeholders seriously. You could argue Standard Chartered Bank has been practising stakeholder engagement since 1853, entrenching itself in some of the most difficult, but also most endearing markets on the planet, with a remarkable long-term commitment. That is one of the things that sets the Bank apart from most international peers. I was sure I was going to learn a lot – and I have.

The time also coincides with a period when several banks around the world, including Standard Chartered Bank, were penalised by regulators with conduct fines. The industry had to tighten up, triggering a series of 'business conduct remediation' programmes. Following the Global Financial Crisis (GFC) and the European debt crisis, we can reflect now on over a decade of 'desert crossing'.

We witnessed most international banks going through, with varying degrees of success, a combination of balance sheet and conduct of business remediation, all of which was existential. But it also created a more risk-averse culture in the industry, antagonising at times the 'business' and 'risk' departments, and inducing an 'internally focused' way of conducting business.

Yet, clients all over the Bank's footprint needed financial services more than ever. They needed funding for growth and help managing complex cross-border risks, while policymakers wanted financial inclusion, jobs, and technology transfers. I am describing a dichotomy between clients and societies needing their banks, and the banks focusing a lot on themselves, understandably in the context of having to survive.

Standard Chartered Bank has always been at the centre of this tension. It is a sophisticated international organisation, accountable to its regulators, and for the delivery of financial and strategic objectives to equally sophisticated shareholders. At the same time, it is anchored – both financially and emotionally – in some of the fastest growing, but also most complex markets in the world.

Starting in 2015, the Bank embarked on a strategy with three components: securing its foundations, becoming lean and focused, and investing and innovating. These objectives were about managing risks, improving efficiency, driving growth and profitability, and they have progressed well over the years.

However, there was also a firm belief that banks of the future will look very different from the banks of today. In late 2017, we realised we needed something more to drive transformation in our industry and bridge the gap that had appeared between banks and the communities they were supposed to serve. If we did not transform the business of banking ourselves, someone else would do it for us.

So, we set out to reconcile that disconnect by 'rewiring the DNA in banking', to serve existing and new clients differently. This was going to take technology, partnerships and different ways of

Preface

operating the business at times – hence an element of change, and transformation of culture and mindset – in other words the 'DNA in banking'.

A lot of the necessary 'genetic code' was already there:

- The links Standard Chartered Bank has to its footprint, the goodwill in the hearts and minds of thousands of corporations and individuals who need a bank with its particular breadth and depth of capabilities.

- A mindset of partnerships: big enough to matter, in some of the fastest growing markets in the world, but not so big (or arrogant) that we could not be a good partner for others, including smaller or very different companies.

- The Bank's understanding of what it takes to operate in dynamic regulated environments, whereas new entrants may not know what they do not know – again an opportunity for partnerships. The trust inspired by a 'bank grade' ventures business has proven to be differentiating in the eyes of clients and regulators, and more than outweighs the costs of being backed by a bank that until recently, was better known for focusing primarily on old economy clients.

Concurrent with the formation of SC Ventures, the Bank was also starting to think about how to use its unique abilities to connect capital, people, ideas, and best practices to help address some of the most significant socio-economic challenges and opportunities of our time: the existential risks from climate change, social division created by rising inequality, and threats to international co-operation that maintain peace and social stability.

Conversely, the businesses funded and developed by SC Ventures have also become important in such pursuits:

- Helping emerging markets in our footprint reduce carbon emissions as fast as possible, without slowing development, putting the world on a sustainable path to net zero by 2050.

- Unleashing the full potential of women and small businesses in our footprint to improve the lives of millions of people and their communities.

- Supporting hundreds of thousands of companies to improve working and environmental standards, giving more people the chance to participate in the world economy, so growth becomes fairer and more balanced.

These objectives were represented from the outset in the investment themes of SC Ventures.

This book lays out the early challenges we faced transforming the Bank – one intrapreneur, one partnership, or one venture at a time – but at the same time we realised how powerful our platform and culture could be.

The inspiration for a book came about as I was contemplating the ups and the downs of our journey – from the seeds planted in 2016 and the incorporation of SC Ventures that began in earnest in 2018 – plus the many learnings along the way. As September 2024, the SC Ventures core platform has grown to approximately 120 people and almost 2,000 across incubating and commercial ventures, as well as digital banks, coalescing around three principal activities: innovation and intrapreneurs, corporate venture capital investment, and creating optionality for banking through the creation of new ventures.

As we engaged many banks and clients for partnering on new business models, we also realised how distinct SC Ventures was. Many large corporates have some sort of venture capital arm, and some even have an innovation lab, but very few have a venture-building capability, let alone all three under one roof. I remember a conversation with a rival global financial institution, after learning how we were set up and how far we came in such a short time, asking, "How did you have the stomach to do this?" I have found myself explaining our model time and time again, which was also another reason to put pen to paper.

This book was written as we have gone from 'zero to one' in over five years. The foundations have been laid, and new working cultural norms are taking root. Yet, we are only getting started,

Preface   xvii

there is so much more to come. As such, what is shared here is but a snapshot in time.

As with any endeavour, this book would not have been possible without the efforts of the contributors. As we uphold diversity in SC Ventures, the book reflects their journeys and views – not only mine. We have purposely maintained their differences in writing style, which gives rise to a series of connected essays rather than just one narrative, presented through a single lens, by a lone author. Through this multi-lens approach, we also hope to convey and celebrate the very diversity of thought that has been the cornerstone of innovation and creative success in SC Ventures. I hope you enjoy this uncut view.

The success of SC Ventures and innovation efforts across many areas of the Bank hinges on collaboration, on it being much 'greater than the sum of its parts'. These parts include our many partners across Standard Chartered Bank, who along with SC Ventures members, are often working outside of the limelight, and yet help drive us forward, each and every day. To all of our partners and those members of SC Ventures, I say thank you. Lastly, I hope this book can contribute in some small way to those other corporate venture arms as they embark on or continue similar journeys so that they can reap successes while navigating the multitude of challenges that corporate innovation will always face.

Alex Manson
CEO, SC Ventures

1

THE GENESIS OF SC VENTURES

Alex Manson

CEO, SC Ventures

"SC Ventures grew from the idea of making ourselves more relevant to the growth and sustainability of our markets."

LAYING THE FOUNDATIONS FOR 'BANKING THE ECOSYSTEM'

In his book *Connect*, Sir John Browne reflected on the historically fractured relationship between business and society throughout history, from Chinese merchants to the Global Financial Crisis (GFC), including Chicago meatpackers and the Deepwater Horizon disaster, and argued that the dawn of artificial intelligence is likely triggering a range of massive labour market dislocations, hence the focus needed to be not just on Corporate and Social Responsibility (CSR) – which is dismissed as almost a distraction – but rather on a much more fundamental approach to this relationship.

By 2015, I was becoming convinced that the banking industry was losing its way. Banks were focusing on themselves instead of their customers. In the post-GFC period, many banks had lost their pioneering spirit, and had become overly process-driven and risk-averse. Our clients needed us to be there for them, to address their pressing needs, finance their economic growth, or help increase their well-being. They wanted us to serve them in the ways they needed. Yet, as an industry, global banks seemed to have lost that fundamental relationship with customers.

Then within the Bank, I advocated an initiative called 'Banking the Ecosystem'. The idea was driven by conversations with clients about their supply chains, in markets like Nigeria or Pakistan. It is difficult for large multinational corporations to convince their international suppliers to operate in such regions, as well as balance their domestic suppliers to cope with growth, and for their distributors to finance their inventory in these territories.

'Banking the Ecosystem' was a way to address these challenges holistically by treating customers not as individual entities, but as an ecosystem of entities. For example, for a bank to serve large company X well, it should also ideally support X's entire ecosystem, so that it might graduate from the role of 'service provider' to become an indispensable 'partner'. There are some important technological implications of this: the use of banking mobile applications in a supply chain; the universal use of data to enable underwriting; the integration of physical, informational and financial flows. But the main point was to reconnect banking and society by making ourselves more relevant to the growth and sustainability of our markets.

By 2017, 'Banking the Ecosystem' was a strategic initiative for Standard Chartered Bank. It had quickly become part of our narrative. In the first year, about half of our new commercial or small and medium-sized enterprise (SME) bank clients had come from this initiative. We were also achieving the plan, roughly on par with our financial metrics, and exceeding the non-financial ones. The problem was that the plan was not good enough. Growing this part of the Bank's business somewhere between five and ten percent may have been a fine outcome, but if we believed that the opportunity was to build the greatest SME business in Asia, then it was not meeting the goal. I had hoped to pulverise our targets with 'exponential growth', but this was not happening.

There were two factors for this. First is that in any large organisation, it is difficult to align new global initiatives across multiple markets and businesses where there are competing priorities. Working within a matrix organisation where there are many different customers, products and regions accentuates this phenomenon. This is also

The Genesis of SC Ventures

a cultural point. I simply underestimated the challenges inherent in an organisation spread across multiple markets, each with its own dynamics, all at a distance from headquarters. Processes are normally well defined across different markets, to enable consistency at scale and changing them implies that people will expect very clear directions from the top before they can align to a new initiative.

Second, and more technically, we were using the Bank's 'old tools', specifically, those related to client onboarding and credit underwriting, as opposed to tools enabling data-driven ecosystem analysis. This was partly for good reasons: our models were proven, and explicitly approved by regulators. Changing the tools would be a lengthy process.

Accordingly, when proposing to our risk officers that they adopt a new model, their instinctive reaction would be: "Sure, let me try it in parallel while I continue doing things the same way and over time we'll see if it works" (this is 'belts and suspenders', essentially implying we have multiple layers of controls before allowing any changes). While belts and suspenders can be viewed as safe and conservative, it is also not pretty and in our analogy, constrains the rigidity that innovation demands.

Against this backdrop, the idea occurred to me to try this innovation again, but outside the Bank. It would be positioned as an independent venture, or platform, with independent governance. So, I pitched the idea of ventures to our CEO, Bill Winters, who had also been reflecting for some time on the subject of innovation and transformation of banking.

Our conversation went something like this:

BILL: *It is the Bank I need to transform. Are you telling me that we can't drive such initiatives from within the Bank?*

ALEX: In a nutshell, yes – while large parts of the Bank need to transform from within, there are initiatives which need to take a fundamentally different approach, even potentially compete with the core business. 'Banking the Ecosystem' won't work within the Bank; we tried, failed and even think we understand why we failed. It needs to be outside.

BILL: *What I'm really after is transforming THIS Bank. You've done TB (Transaction Banking) for long enough, how*

> *about being a Chief Innovation Officer, leading the bank's innovation and transformation agenda – most corporates have one these days?*

ALEX: I have to say, these innovation jobs typically fail or disappoint ... In any event, a former consultant or strategist would be much better at this, not a business guy. But if you open up to the possibility of ventures, then the innovation might take care of itself.

It was arrogant of me to say this, as nothing ever takes care of itself in business. Yet, in this conversation, we laid the first foundation for SC Ventures and how it might transform the Bank. Our conversation continued over several sessions.

Bill asked me a lot of challenging questions related to culture change across the broader organisation – how will we achieve that if we are doing innovation 'outside the Bank'? We also debated whether the digital agenda of the retail or corporate Bank was in scope for this role (hint: it shouldn't!). How should we approach the topic of fintech investments, which many corporate venture capitalists (CVCs) were doing?

There was broad alignment of vision and then came a more challenging conversation:

BILL: *I've been exposed to people who made a fortune spinning off valuable assets of their enterprise and the firm got nothing for it. I'm not saying that this is what you have in mind (you wouldn't be anywhere close to this conversation if I thought you did), but I still can't let that happen.*

ALEX: Basically, you're telling me that you don't want me within the Ventures, but on the Bank's payroll, looking after the Bank?

BILL: *Yes, watching after the interests of the broader Bank.*

ALEX: Are we clear that the CEOs of ventures will need to be incentivised differently, meaning equity in the ventures? They need to live and die by their venture!

BILL: *Yes.*

ALEX: Okay. So, we're saying I'm not the CEO of these things, but something like the head of a portfolio of ventures.

> The CEO gets paid as a function of the success of the venture, whereas I get paid what you think is right, correct?

BILL: *Yes. But you will also need to help change the Bank. I'm serious about the innovation role. You will need to prioritise disruptive things – joint ventures, partnerships, different types of businesses, which the Bank couldn't do by itself.*

This conversation cemented my faith. Bill had the courage to allow me to take a different approach than most organisations had in the past, and certainly not many in banking. At the same time, he ensured that whatever we did was in the broader interests of the Bank and accelerating its transformation agenda. Most CEOs struggle to strike a balance between driving change and seeking consensus and harmony around such change. They also typically rely on their existing teams to create change and may be afraid of breaking anything. This was different.

I struck that deal because my objective was to make the Ventures happen. In my view, in the context of banking, the risk of doing nothing was far higher than that of breaking a fence or two. By the way, I was equally serious about innovation in the Bank itself, however, I did not think a conventional approach would ever work, and this was beginning to look like a much better shot at it.

INVENTING SC VENTURES

During our following conversations, Bill and I invented a new unit of the Bank, to be called 'SC Ventures'. It would include the eXellerator lab, which had been spearheading innovation in the Bank with fintech engagement. It would also involve a human-centred design (HCD) curriculum, and SC Studios – a small scouting office in San Francisco. We wanted to design a way to invest in the fintech ecosystem. The eXellerator, the Innovation Investment Fund and the Ventures became the 'three pillars' of SC Ventures, which we launched in March 2018.

An interesting question at this juncture is why we combined different activities, with full knowledge of the fact that these 'pillars' were likely to fail or disappoint when taken individually.

First, my initial reaction to the 'innovation job' Bill mentioned had been that I probably would not last very long. Why? Innovation projects typically fail because they are marginal for the corporate and can only have so much alignment with business units. Even when they are extremely well co-ordinated, agendas are necessarily very different. Such labs are typically positioned as an 'internal consultant' or 'agent of change', helping others in their evolution, or digitisation efforts, as opposed to a 'principal' project that has the resources (including capital) to create change. Often the head of innovation becomes a 'priest' of some sort, someone on a mission to evangelise the rest of the organisation until the corporation becomes tired of listening, and the priest becomes tired of preaching.

Second, building ventures is challenging: they are startups, implying that they are small – initially too small to matter to larger core businesses. In fact, in a corporation that is building and incubating ventures, they are designed to be this way. They are, by their very nature, small business experiments. This takes nothing away from the learning experience you gain from building them. It also does not rule out that some of the ventures could become large and profitable businesses over time, but it is unlikely to happen immediately. This makes them difficult to support from the position of business units under pressure to produce immediate results at scale.

Lastly, some corporations, including banks, have been investing in startups for a long time. Everything from an integrated 'strategic investor' model, where all investments are closely tied to the corporate activity, to completely separate private equity or venture capital (VC) style operations. We will look later at why these efforts typically fail or disappoint, but for now, it is sufficient to say that such small investments – typically minority stakes in typically subscale vendors – generally do not have any notable transformational impact on the business, they are too small to matter. Such investment business can be successful in its own right, but it is unclear how much the corporation gets out of it and therefore, they are little more than a distraction.

So, one might ask: if labs fail to bring about change, investments are a distraction, and ventures are generally too small to matter, why bother? To which the answer is: that the combination of all three might have a transformational impact. In designing SC

The Genesis of SC Ventures

7

Ventures and its three pillars, we were betting that while any one of the efforts would be insufficient to have a transformational impact by itself, the combination of the three actually *would*.

First, the flow of information is extremely powerful. Use cases in a corporate environment can give birth to new venture ideas; hidden gems neglected as a utility could become businesses in their own right if repositioned commercially (think of Amazon Web Services emerging from within Amazon); and people in the organisation provide the first source of talent that can be redeployed into the ventures themselves (a real advantage, although not without its traps).

Second, the ventures allow the organisation to experiment safely and cheaply. They can prove or disprove a point. After some time, the corporation has the option to reabsorb the venture by buying it out, or it can completely sever ties with it, replicate it inside the corporation, or take on only some of its practices. In other words, it provides a series of strategic options. Options are important to gather, as an option premium is relatively small compared to its (uncertain) payout. In other words, the corporation buys options on alternative business models, but it does not have to commit to such business models.

It is easy to see how there is a two-way flow between the organisation and its ventures, even when they are kept independent from each other, so that they can provide the necessary choices. Additionally, an investment effort helps cement partnerships, both in the context of internal transformation efforts and in the ventures. The numbers do not need to be high; in fact, they probably should not be, as the investment effort is not meant to become a large business itself. It is a means to an end: the end again being transformational impact, in our case, through fintech partnerships.

When SC Ventures was announced in 2018, I do not think that any bank had genuinely combined these activities under one roof with such intended flows of information and people. Typically, banks have 'labs' (as described above) and many have investment efforts, sometimes a number of them are scattered in different places. Very few finance industry ventures are built outside of its core business, perhaps because they would have been small distractions or because of regulatory concerns. The banks that came closest at the time were ING, Santander and BBVA, all three well respected in the context of innovation and with established investment practices (in fact, my first trip on the job was to Madrid and Amsterdam to learn from these banks' experiences).

INSEAD – BUSINESS AS A FORCE FOR GOOD

In 2022 we were shortlisted by INSEAD as a top three finalist in the *Business as a Force for Good Award*. We presented how SC Ventures is playing its part in fulfilling society's expectations of banking and finance. It was also a reflection on how we are contributing to our wider mission in rewiring the DNA in banking and a proud moment in our journey.

TAKEAWAYS

- The banking industry risks being irrelevant in today's environment and therefore losing relevance with its clients.
- There needs to be a new way of rethinking the industry and approaching innovations.
- In designing SC Ventures and its three pillars, we created something unique. Just one of the pillars would be insufficient, but the combination of all three would achieve the desired transformation.

2

CATALYSING INTERNAL INNOVATION

Alex Manson

CEO, SC Ventures

"What do you mean when you say — innovation is every-one's job — if you genuinely believe innovation is every-one's job, across all ranks, as we did ..."

LAUNCHING SC INNOVATE AND THE INTRAPRENEURS PROGRAMME

Most innovation programmes start with a statement along the lines of: "Innovation is everyone's job". They often begin with leaders soliciting ideas and initiatives from their enthusiastic staff. An exciting selection process follows, and initiatives are launched. However, in many cases, these initiatives fail to blossom as interest wanes either through lack of support or because other projects take precedence.

Yet, it is a fact that no organisation can transform itself without involving most of its employees in one way or another. The problem is how – how to sustain momentum and how to translate that momentum into genuine transformation.

We took the view that we would involve people by fostering an entrepreneurial culture within the Bank through our Intrapreneurs Programme. For this initiative to be sustainable, we needed to create momentum and importantly, maintain this by the 'crowd' (as opposed to top-down directives). Finally, for the initiative to have a transformational impact, we knew that it needed to be all about skills building – not just entrepreneurial skills, but also design skills – the ability to think of client problems differently, and to solve them through the innovative use of technology. In other words, while ideas can be important, the work we are doing is ultimately about skills, mindset and culture. We are working on the DNA of the organisation, one intrapreneur at a time.

Similar initiatives were happening concurrently, elsewhere within the Bank. A relatively recently arrived Chief Operating Officer (COO) started introducing 'new ways of working'. At the same time, the Retail business unit was investing more (increasingly senior individuals and ever-larger investment budgets) in 'digitising the Bank'. While the Corporate and Investment Banking (CIB) unit created a 'Digital Channel and Data Analytics' (DCDA) group that was building on the 'next generation channels', that we had built in Transaction Banking (TB).

If you genuinely believe that 'innovation is everyone's job', as we did, then centralising such efforts, or even attempting to co-ordinate them, is completely nonsensical. Like-minded people contributed in their ways, sometimes this was incremental contributions – which is equally important – and sometimes more transformational. The tools applied might differ slightly, but all held the common threads of agility and customer-centric design.

FROM TB INNOVATE TO SC INNOVATE

The Intrapreneurs Programme started in TB of Standard Chartered Bank. We designed TB Innovate, a platform designed for people to submit ideas on anything from client propositions to product development, with the crowd in TB commenting and voting on the ideas. The success of the programme was both evident and mixed. It was evident because people did engage with it. They submitted genuinely thoughtful propositions, some of which we implemented.

Catalysing Internal Innovation

This created little bits of homegrown innovation in the unit. It was also mixed because it was usually the same individuals who engaged – the like-minded ones, who typically sat together in a corner of the Singapore floor. (Presumably, the message never really made it to people elsewhere in the Bank.)

The platform was branded with its logo, consisting of a little cube reminiscent of the logo we used to communicate TB's priorities. When it was presented at the CIB management team meeting, the interim head of that unit liked it so much that he initially suggested renaming 'TB Innovate' as 'CIB Innovate', before he corrected himself: "Of course, this should be SC Innovate." The little cube remained on the logo for a while, as a souvenir.

SC Innovate is underlaid by two main assumptions:

- The crowd might know something management does not. Would it not be great if those bankers who engage with clients or experience the latest technologies were the ones telling management what the next innovation should be? In fact, the crowd might know more than management does. Rather than managers making autocratic decisions on how to prioritise investments, could we experiment with an environment where the crowd voted and outlined the next priorities?

- We would all gain by empowering those people who were willing just to get on with things, rather than telling them what to do. We were trying to move away from a top-down 'chain of command' and to allow small groups of individuals to do what they thought was right, provided they had support from their peers on the platform.

The more managers tell people what to do, the more employees expect to be told what to do, and so become 'internally and process-focused' rather than taking the initiative.

In this case, the boss plays the role of the boss, telling people what to do, and the junior takes the role of a junior banker, obediently following directions. However, in order to perform at our best, let alone transform anything, we need professionals to step out of their role-play and embrace the whole enterprise. To foster innovation and creation, we certainly need junior bankers and all ranks in the organisation to be 'intrapreneurial': to do what they know is right for clients. This requires the bosses to step out of their conventional roles: rather than telling others what to do, they should provide a platform where people can do what they think is the right thing – and innovate. This is easier said than done, and by far the hardest thing for a leader to do, is to unlearn their reflexes and resist the urge to 'help' their team by instructing them on what to do.

In other words, the more management focuses on a shared purpose – a 'North Star' or a clear goal – while allowing employees to identify the steps for themselves, the more initiative they can come to expect and, over time, deliver greater results. A sense of ownership will add motivation and energy, which more than makes up for the occasional duplication or efficiency loss.

> *"The added motivation and energy generated by the sense of ownership more than makes up for the occasional duplication or efficiency loss."*

THE INTRAPRENEURS PROGRAMME

We designed the Intrapreneurs Programme to allow people to spend 20 percent of their time working on their own projects – a concept borrowed from the famous Google example. First, they would submit a project or idea to the SC Innovate platform. The 'crowd', rather than management, would then vote on projects and decide which ones were worth pursuing. At this point we would form a small team: typically, the individual(s) who submitted, along with subject-matter experts from the Bank (legal, compliance or technology). We would bring a method and tools, basically combining human-centred design (HCD) with a 'Lean Startup' approach to encourage the teams to articulate a Minimum Viable Product (MVP). We then would test it immediately and tweak it based on feedback. We repeat this process again, and again and again. Obviously, we did not invent any of these methods; they are in fact so well known, they constitute 'buzz words' in the world of business innovation consultants. Yet, what struck us was that they are rarely used at scale in conventional corporations (other than

Catalysing Internal Innovation 13

in the remote innovation labs). Taking them mainstream was a big opportunity.

The saying goes that successful startups are not those with the best idea or technology, but the ones that iterate the most (literally, the greatest number of times, meaning try, get feedback, adjust, try again, etc.), so we wanted to start integrating that concept in the Bank's 'ways of working'. Once the MVP was sufficiently iterated, a prototype was presented to a 'Dragon's Den' composed of business unit managers. Here, funding for implementation might be granted or the initiative might be integrated into an existing product line or working group.

Our first global intrapreneur challenge was met with mixed success. The final selection process was difficult. Also, we started looking too late for business sponsors – only after the teams had created a prototype. Additionally, the challenge of being able to use 20 percent of one's time to work on an intrapreneur idea is very difficult to manage in the real world. We were fortunate that many of our intrapreneurs were willing to work in their own time to gain experience and exposure, as they sometimes lacked support from their middle managers.

To address some of these issues, we now engage with business sponsors and craft problem statements together before we open a 'challenge'. This allows for later selection of ideas by people vested in the project, as well as for a commitment that serious consideration will be given to implementation at scale should the ideas succeed. It also made us more comfortable with early funding for the teams so they could research and build their prototypes before pitching.

FLASH FORWARD

The Intrapreneurs Programme is now a more structured process, with regular communications, connections with our offices around the world, connections to business subject-matter experts, and support from the SC Ventures team where needed. We still have not cracked the 20 percent innovation time allocation, but we have come a long way and are working with the Bank to ensure that our intrapreneurs' efforts are recognised.

HAVE INTRAPRENEURS ALREADY CHANGED THE BANK?

We tend to second-guess ourselves on just about everything, so this is a fair question. Like with everything else, if it is not contributing to 'rewiring the DNA in banking', then we should not do it! The programme is 'satisfying', as we can see the immediate results with individuals and their new ideas implemented, yet it is harder to assess the overall long-term impact on the organisation. Our conviction, though, is that the programme has had an impact, by evidence of the sheer number of ideas submitted and worked on, and the large number of people involved. The way to think of it, is as skills building, one intrapreneur at a time. We are doing to the organisation what an evolving athlete does to their body: developing and training new muscles to be able to compete in a new kind of race.

CardsPal is a great example of intrapreneurs gone entrepreneurs – meaning, in this case, Venture Leads. When we first saw 'Credit Card Buddy', it was a project within the Bank and for the Bank, led by enthusiastic participants in the programme who had pitched their idea of a credit card benefit app for the Bank. However, a few months into it, we realised that while banks were keen to extend credit card benefits to consumers to induce more sign-ups, they were not necessarily incentivised to help users optimise or redeem such benefits. Also, and perhaps more importantly, being outside the Bank was the only way to make it clear to potential partners that we were a genuinely open bank, as well as bank-agnostic.

TAKEAWAYS

- Innovation is everyone's job. Everyone says that – what do you mean by that and how do you enable everyone's job to innovate in a large corporate organisation?
- There is an untapped talent within organisations; people who have an entrepreneurial spirit but want the safety of a corporation to test and experiment.

3

CARDSPAL: CREDIT CARD REWARDS MADE EASY

Saim Yeong Harng

Previous CEO, CardsPal

CardsPal is a credit cards rewards aggregator, incubated through the SC Ventures platform, and sold to Utu, a travel technology firm in 2023.

"DO or DO NOT; there is no TRY."

CardsPal in a nutshell: CardsPal discovers credit card deals, rewards, discounts and offers to help you maximise your savings and earn back cash on your credit cards. We aggregate all vendors and merchants so that you never miss out on opportunities. Manage all your credit cards in one place, and never miss a deal again.

CardsPal's vision: CardsPal's vision is to be the largest and most trusted online data-driven personal finance marketplace. CardsPal was driven by a problem that I faced. With multiple cards, most of the time I had difficulty choosing which card to use to maximise my savings. CardsPal was born when I realised the benefits of an app that could aggregate all my cards' deals and show eligible nearby ones.

CardsPal's mission: CardsPal's mission is to make people's life easier by helping them effortlessly discover the best nearby deals and financial instruments. We deploy user-centric design thinking and a data-driven approach powered by machine learning to create a hyper-personalised experience for our users.

CardsPal's landing page: utu.global[1]

THE DRIVE TO BUILD

What if you had the opportunity to turn your idea into a reality and leave your mark on the world? Working in the corporate world for over a decade made me reluctant to kick-start my dream of being an entrepreneur, of following a vision that ignites my passion. Although I knew there would never be a better time to step out of my comfort zone into building a venture, there was a lot of self-doubt about making this dream a reality and building a successful business. As someone neither risk-averse nor risk-seeking, I still had an entrepreneurial seed inside me. Yet, without any external events pushing me, there was no desire to grow that seed. That is, until 2018.

In 2018, SC Ventures organised its first Global Intrapreneur Challenge. It proved to be the external force I needed to germinate the seed of entrepreneurship, and I started a journey that would transform my life. Out of over 400 innovative ideas submitted, mine was shortlisted through several preliminary stages and eventually made it to the finals – the Dragon's Den.

This is also when I met my mentor, Gautam Jain. Gautam provided advice and guidance that helped me navigate the unique situation and complexities of building a venture in the corporate world. This mentorship, forged at the very beginning of my journey, was the second external factor that paved the way for my later successes.

My DNA was rewired the moment my idea was selected in the Dragon's Den and I was given the title 'Intrapreneur'. It brought me nearer to the dream of building a venture, and I was thrilled. I knew I could make a difference, and that my passion would help me to sail through any obstacles. My entrepreneurial seed sprouted and I was up for the next big challenge, which was to create a proof of concept (POC).

FROM EMPLOYEE TO INTRAPRENEUR

As I was still working full-time at the beginning of my intrapreneurship, the start of this process was not easy. As well as the 20 percent of my work hours that I could use to focus on my new initiative, I spent most of my evenings and weekends on meeting milestones. Juggling both streams of work was demanding, but I had the energy to push through it, with support from the team around me. I was also motivated by a strong belief that my hard work would pay off. My motto is that the biggest regret in life is not when we tried and failed; it is when we never tried. Even if my idea did not make the cut, I knew I would have no regrets.

I was not familiar on how to transform an idea into a venture. I had a clearer idea of what was needed to pitch for POC funding after attending training at the intrapreneur boot camp; I had a clearer picture of what I needed. This was to strengthen the business model by applying the business model canvas; building a prototype and validating the business idea to prove it was worth pursuing.

Time was in short supply and it was important to keep the momentum going. My POC funding was approved and I was onto the next stage. This means conducting marketing research and getting the resources together to build the prototype. It felt great to tick off another milestone on my checklist and a step closer to my goal.

My intrapreneur coach, Kelvin Tan, guided me on how to craft a great pitch deck and shared his contacts (senior leaders of the Bank and subject-matter experts) to whom I could reach out to validate the idea and business model.

Richard Lu volunteered to help me build the prototype. Quiet, humble, creative and responsible, he is a product designer with a great eye for detail. During brainstorming sessions for the design and process flow, I was astonished by how well he could translate my idea into a great design concept. He is a craftsman. I was also amazed by how quickly he could improve his design and come up with an even better one. It was a successful collaboration and I believed we could achieve great results together. I had found my own Jony Ive of Apple.

After two months of preparation, now armed with a prototype, favourable market research and validation, and a refined pitch deck, I was ready for the next challenge.

PRE-SEED FUNDING STAGE

April 2019 was a key milestone for me: I pitched my idea to Brain-Trust (internal VC of Standard Chartered Bank chaired by the Group Chief Information Officer – and gained pre-seed funding of USD$240,000 to build a Minimum Viable Product (MVP). This meant that I could move into SC Ventures to focus on the venture full-time. When Alex Manson asked if I was willing to leave my existing job, I said 'Yes' without any hesitation. This kick-started the next phase of my exciting journey in venture building. There is nothing more fun than having the opportunity to build something you strongly believe in, that can change people's lives, be it in savings, lifestyle, finances or anything else.

> *"There is nothing more fun than having the opportunity to build something you strongly believe in that can change people's lives."*

I shifted into combat mode, focusing first on resourcing. I needed to make several hires immediately as onboarding would take time. This meant deciding when to work with vendors, hire agency contractors or source the resources internally. I adopted a hybrid hiring approach to maximise the outcome and reduce the risk. Through reaching out to my previous teammate, I found talented graduates of the Bank to support with designing the technology stack. As many things were happening at once, and I had crucial decisions to make, this was a steep learning curve. However, I had plenty of support from the team around me – especially my incubator, Thorsten Neumann. I got my scrum team ready: a product and user interface/user experience (UI/UX) designer, a front-end developer, a back-end developer and a data analyst. The venture was born!

We used a lean startup model to build the MVP. We adopted cutting-edge cloud technology to build a scalable technology stack. We brainstormed ideas, created user journeys, designed, validated with users, built, tested and deployed. We ran scrum sessions, and we learnt, improved and iterated. Fortunately, we did not need to deal with a legacy system, due to the nature of the venture. We moved fast and learnt even faster.

Did everything go smoothly without any challenges or obstacles? No. We had some pretty tough hurdles and there were hard decisions to make to keep the venture going. These experiences have enriched my worldview and broadened my horizons. I can now look at things from different angles and the perspective of a leader.

WHAT ARE WE BUILDING?

We are building a platform, a retail mobile application that helps our users to choose the best card to use when purchasing from a merchant or online. It shows nearby personalised and eligible deals powered by machine learning. *CardsPal* is the brand name of the app.

- **Cards** represent the physical or virtual cards that people carry or store in their e-wallet. This includes debit cards, credit cards, loyalty cards, or any other card types that come with rewards and/or deals.

- **Pal** represents a 'friend', 'buddy' or 'mate' who can help to improve the card user's lifestyle by maximising their savings or minimising missed deals.

Using nearby deals as an entry point to drive attribution was novel and not yet established in the Singapore market at the time of writing. We were able to collaborate with banks, merchants, fintech partners and network partners to build capabilities that help them to drive traffic and deals, or to acquire offerings. We have worked hard to build a data-driven, neutral and unbiased platform. These feed into our bigger vision: to build the largest and most trusted online data-driven personal finance marketplace.

One of the many lessons I learned during my venture journey is that entrepreneurial spirit is not about the idea. It is about passion, optimism and agility. It is said that you will never work a single day in your life if you are passionate about what you are doing. Optimism is important because the venture journey can be extremely tough. You will hardly progress if you lose sight of the vision. A small venture has the advantages of being agile, being able to move fast and being easier to pivot if necessary. Understanding and being able to shift quickly to take advantage of market trends will help us to win the race.

SEED FUNDING STAGE

We strongly believe that if an egg is broken by an outside force, life ends; if it is broken by an inside force, life begins. We always wanted to break it from within. While beta-launch gave us some satisfaction in seeing our product reach internal users, it also meant facing our next challenge: launching it to the public. To do this, we would need seed funding. Using our lessons so far and refining our ideas and business model, I readied myself for another pitch.

> *"We strongly believe that if an egg is broken by an outside force, life ends; if it's broken by an inside force, life begins. We always wanted to break it from within."*

We faced more challenging questions during the seed funding round of BrainTrust. Some of the feedback for our business idea was supportive, while other comments were thought provoking and generated valuable new insights. Our pitch was successful, and we received US$1.8 million for this next stage. This major milestone meant a lot to me personally, as it represented CardsPal's readiness to move into a new and more exciting phase. It was time to switch gears and focus on getting the venture off the ground. This meant building a great team to speed up the development of our capabilities, data analytics, user growth, and content creation. It was also important to focus on how quickly we could create the network effect by leveraging on our backer's strength and partnership.

THE LAUNCH (DURING COVID)

We officially launched the CardsPal app in June 2020 during COVID. It was a huge challenge for the team to shift from working next to each other to working remotely with a laptop. We learnt to collaborate virtually, and with determination and perseverance, we were able to achieve a lot of our key milestones.

Team building is part of the equation in venture building. I am particularly careful in selecting my team members. I want to ensure that the environment and culture are conducive, yet not too comfortable, for the team to grow and contribute to the venture. I believe that if we want to grow quickly, we need to be uncomfortable with what we are doing. If we are too comfortable, we are not growing at speed. When hiring, I am always looking to align the personal goals of team members with the venture's vision. I am blessed to be surrounded by a team of great people who work tirelessly, and who are willing to go far and together with me in this venture.

WHAT IS NEXT FOR CARDSPAL?

I envisage people who use the platform achieve their savings and financial goals. They have a tool at their fingertips that means they can enjoy what they are eligible for, and never miss out on a great deal. They only receive the information they are interested in. They love the user interface and seamless experience of the platform. CardsPal allows them to conduct transactions, share their favourite deals with others, and manage their finances. CardsPal is part of their life and they become ambassadors for the brand.

The future is indeed very exciting. A venture that can understand users' psychology well and can quickly and efficiently deliver the experience they want, will win the race. We will continue to co-create this venture with our users and aim to become their top choice.

FINAL THOUGHTS

I am grateful for the opportunity to become an intrapreneur. To borrow Clayton Christensen's terminology, as explained in his book, *How Will You Measure Your Life?*, this is an emergent strategy from an unanticipated opportunity. It has now become my new deliberate strategy. I truly enjoy every moment I spend leading and running this venture with a bunch of diverse, young, energetic and talented people. The opportunity given to me to write this chapter has also brought back a lot of warm memories.

We have accomplished a great deal, and a lot more work lies ahead. We will never set limits or put constraints on what we can do. Together, we can – and will – create miracles.

> *"DO or DO NOT; there is no TRY. As I have chosen the 'DO', the only way forward for me is to continue to lead the team on this challenging, yet exhilarating journey."*

TAKEAWAYS

- Take care of your people, and your people will take care of you.
- Be kind.
- Never give up!

NOTE

1. Link to Utu website as Carsdpal was acquired by Utu Global

4

THE eXELLERATOR: WELCOMING STARTUPS WITH EMPATHY

Alex Manson

CEO, SC Ventures

"What we create together is ours."

Most innovation labs do engage with startups as they hope to learn, take on the best practices, rejuvenate their organisation, and find partnerships that can scale. Yet most corporations are doomed to fail in these objectives because of the way their organisation is set up, the policies they use, and the incentives of the people involved.

For a meaningful and productive relationship, we need to reinvent how corporations engage with startups. Usually, it takes a lab to sit in the middle of a startup and organisation. They also need to work on how the organisation onboards the startup and deals with risk management and intellectual property (IP) negotiations. But most importantly, it takes empathy.

ENGAGING WITH FINTECHS

Any innovation team in a financial institution wants to engage with what we call the 'fintech ecosystem'. Banks will set up labs – ours was originally called the eXellerator – to welcome startups. Then we complete a proof of concept (POC) with the fintech, which in turn creates a whole industry of labs, consultants and startups. The end goal is to transform these initial startups into a sustainable and financeable book of business.

The first problem is that completing the proof of concept is not the same as moving a new product into production. Unfortunately, the more the lab is disconnected from the business units, the less likely it is that the new product will make it to production mode. Plus, moving into production is no guarantee the startup will scale at the enterprise-wide level. (Generally, it is far from it.)

The second problem is that most large corporations, including big banks, are simply not equipped to deal with startups, in terms of both infrastructure and mindset. Even before you get to the technology needed for the new product, dealing with the Bank as a startup can be summarised in three steps: procurement, legal and documentation, and risk interventions.

Large companies make little distinction between a corporation of the size of Microsoft and a nascent startup when it comes to sending out a Request for Proposal (RFP) to vendors. A small company with perhaps a great idea and capabilities, but little time and resources, would be expected to fill out the same lengthy form with many pages of questions. You could argue that this is 'what it takes to play', but in practice, it eliminates a lot of promising contenders early in the process.

The same applies to legal documentation: complex contracts, also reflecting an 'asymmetric profile' (meaning the terms are typically tilted in favour of the larger corporate), which a keen vendor has no choice but to agree to.

Yet, perhaps the main issue is intellectual property (IP). Or rather the imbalance between the startup and large corporation when it comes to IP. In the corporate world, internal counsel is focused on protecting the corporate's IP but for the startup, the IP is pretty much all they have. So, it is not viable for it to enter into an agreement that does not offer them some protection for what they bring to the table.

Risk considerations tend to build walls around the corporation. These happen for several good reasons (cyber-security, safeguarding of client data, etc.), but they also create a lengthy process of third-party vendor vetting – sometimes lasting six months or more – until all the stars are aligned. The underlying difference in mindset is one of big versus small, established versus nascent, buyer leverage versus lack of choice, powerful versus powerless, 'we know it all' versus 'please try me'.

> *"The underlying difference in mindset is one of big versus small, established versus nascent, buyer leverage versus lack of choice, powerful versus powerless, 'we know it all' versus 'please try me'."*

The reality is that it takes patience and resilience to deal with a large corporation when you are not one yourself, to be up against a culture that is protective of the corporation itself (and typically is reluctant to accept any liability or other form of risk sharing). Importantly, and this is particularly prevalent in large banks, we often have to deal with the 'do it yourself' culture: as large IT departments have grown over the years to be the 'curators' of their (sometimes antiquated) systems, they require a vast number of resources that need to be maintained. This keeps everyone busy, creating a formidable barrier to entry for young startups.

ENGAGING WITH EMPATHY THROUGH A SPECIALLY DESIGNED FRAMEWORK

Taking everything above into account, large banks need to adapt their traditional frameworks when dealing with startups. This will give a more balanced interaction that preserves incentives for both sides to come together. It will also speed up the process and protect the resources of the much smaller – and, hence, less resilient – startup. Empathy is not what you normally expect from a corporate manager, but it is required in this case to ensure that the interaction does not ultimately destroy the culture you are engaging with, and possibly hope to emulate in your organisation. To do this, we need to understand the startup's objective (which in most cases is to survive to its next milestone, typically a round of financing). It could even involve giving away some of the leverage the large corporation typically enjoys to achieve a more balanced relationship.

It certainly involves understanding the startup's expectations, including the fact that there is no point in conducting a POC without a clear and relatively quick path to implementation should it be successful. It also involves appreciating the scarcity of the startup's resources. For example, if they might run out of cash while waiting for the completion of a procurement process (something that is not unheard of), then the right answer from the large firm to even a begging founder is: "Sorry, don't engage with us yet. We would drain you. Come back when you are more resilient and enterprise ready." Saying "No, because…" is far preferable, from a startup's perspective, than "Yes, maybe…", especially if the 'Yes' is motivated (either consciously or subconsciously) by maintaining your options. Honest feedback such as "This doesn't work for us, because…", or "We will ultimately not implement this, because the difference between what we would gain and what we already have is marginal and would not justify the effort", may sound harsh, but it could also encourage the startup to revamp or radically change its product or proposition, making it potentially more appealing in future.

At SC Ventures, we have set ourselves the challenge of getting any POC started within two weeks of engagement, provided the POC did not require the use of real (hence, confidential and protected) client data. We have succeeded in doing this. Lots of POCs can be completed with anonymised or 'dummy' data, allowing a much simpler and shorter onboarding process. Procurement, the business unit responsible for, among other things, dealing with suppliers, getting the best possible deal from them and ensuring they adhere to the firm's standards, will typically have built a sophisticated and lengthy process for selecting suppliers. In the context of a POC, this can be accelerated: the lab is procurement; the price negotiation is all about a fair relationship.

Likewise, the legal and documentation aspects can be greatly simplified and adapted to the needs of a fintech engaging with the bank. If IP is all the startup has, and the bank brings little to the table other than 'observing a POC', there is little point in attempting to protect the bank's IP to the detriment of the startup's. Instead, the balance should be along the lines of: "What you bring to the table on day one is yours. What we create together is ours."

ARE POCS MEANINGLESS?

No, a POC is a proxy for 'engagement'. A company can use a POC to test an idea or a technology. It also allows the validation of a 'use case': does a particular product work to solve a particular problem, assuming the problem is worth solving? Perhaps more importantly, it is in the course of a POC that people get to know each other, building trust both ways (or not!).

PARENTING AN ADOLESCENT STARTUP AND CHOOSING THE RIGHT TIME TO ENGAGE WITH A CORPORATE

Adolescence is a difficult age for a variety of reasons, but it is also an interesting and rewarding time for the open-minded parent. An adolescent child, or 'teen', is old enough to understand a lot of the world around them, yet still perceives it differently from adults, being less constrained by social norms and habits. Teens are old enough to form their own views, which may sometimes be provocative. They are less bound by established ways of doing things and are more prone to invent their own methods or to try out other options. Creative experimentation is the hallmark of adolescence.

Yet, experimentation has downsides: it often involves making mistakes, which can cause parents to feel anxiety. We know that adolescents' brains are not completely formed until they are in their early twenties, so they have less capacity to anticipate and evaluate the consequences of their actions. This explains, in part, the 'recklessness' or formidable risk-seeking behaviour of teens – they are sometimes simply oblivious to the consequences of their actions. Those behaviours also challenge adults, sometimes keeping us honest, or forcing us to consider things from a different perspective.

There is such a thing as being too early – or too late – for engagement. As it relates to a relationship between parents and their teenage children (which can be difficult for all the above reasons), it is likely to be a very formative one. Changing their young child's nappies can be a thrilling parenting experience, but it is hardly a two-way street. (My conversations with my children when they were this age were not the most intellectually stimulating, even leaving aside my sleep-deprived state.) Later in life, young adults can have a thrilling relationship with their parents in the context of shared interests or ongoing family bonds, but it is no longer as formative a relationship as when they were in their teens. A parent can still provide guidance or advice, but the impact of the engagement is limited by the fact that a young adult is old enough to lead their own life and assume responsibility for the consequences of their actions. Adolescence, the age between nappies and young adulthood, is a 'sweet spot' that potentially offers formative, if difficult, experiences with one's children.

Similarly, for large corporations and fintechs, engaging too early can be interesting, but often unproductive. The startup may be able to contribute a good idea and a small team, yet not at the scale, resilience and maturity that is needed to deal with a large corporation in a more long-term, sustainable way. Later in the life of a startup, the relationship can be very productive, yet much less formative. By this stage, a vendor can typically take care of itself and has its own policies, procedures and ways of protecting itself. The mutual contribution is well defined in a commercial agreement that outlines the roles and responsibilities of each party.

Following the analogy above, the 'sweet spot is in between' when the startup is mature enough to make a significant contribution to the corporation. They are enterprise-ready and able to speak the same language, as well as being resilient enough to cope with the bureaucracy and cultural traits of the large firm. At the same time, the startup remains genuinely innovative, not just in terms of its product's IP, but also in its methods of working. This brings diverse cultural traits and ways of thinking that may be lacking in an established corporation.

Like our teens, the startup's risk appetite is typically much higher than that of the corporation. This risk may be appropriate for an entrepreneur starting from nothing but will probably be too high in the context of a business at scale. 'The brain is not yet completely formed'; governance, policies and procedures are not set for everything or can be quite simplistic. This often means improvising and pivoting quickly as a result of ongoing client feedback, but it can be inefficient and overly risky in the context of a business at scale, that requires processes that you can replicate. Sometimes part of the brain is missing – the Chief Financial Officer is not really a CFO; the founder is performing all the main roles; checks and balances are immature; compliance and risk are non-existent.

In exchange for the startup's contribution to the corporation's ability to solve a client problem, innovate, or just rejuvenate, the corporation can provide guidance and learning experiences that will contribute to the startup's ability to survive, and scale to the next stage of its evolution. This is a two-way street and is an eminently formative one, where both parties can genuinely benefit from the relationship, way beyond the narrowly defined terms of the commercial agreements between them.

The place where a lot of this happened was the eXellerator. As mentioned, the eXellerator pre-dated SC Ventures and was essentially an innovation lab. Importantly, this is where we started advocating 'new ways of working', including (but not limited to) human-centred design, agile working, and the lean startup approach. It is also where we engaged with business units, attempting to understand and frame their problems to, ideally, find a solution. That was the demand side of the equation.

On the supply side, the eXellerator is also where we engaged with a multitude of fintechs, several hundred in any one year – sometimes quite superficially (good to know, nothing imminent to pursue) and sometimes quite deeply. In fact, some startups designed their very first use case within our lab before 'scaling on' to a very successful journey. Today, it is very clear to us that our eXellerator was quite different from most labs in the corporate world. The following chapters tell the story of how this happened.

TAKEAWAYS

- You can compare a startup to an adolescent brain. It is still learning, takes more risks and needs guidance.

- The role of the bank is to provide that guidance so that the startup can scale and become a mature business.

- Much can be learned from the experimentation that takes place in a startup environment.

5

THE eXELLERATOR: OLD MEETS NEW

Wea Meng Chang

Previous Operating Member

"These clients now see Standard Chartered Bank as being more than a bank. They see us as a technology builder — a strategic venture partner with whom they can create and test new revenue opportunities."

Many large organisations have innovation labs. They are all set up to look edgy, cool, and nothing like the traditional corporate environment. Yet the intent and conviction that underpins these labs may promise very different results. In the context of an established 160+-year-old bank, operating in an industry that has seen heightened anxiety to explore and test new operating and business models through innovation. These labs are attempting to address the entrenched financial exclusion of millennials, and micro, small and medium-sized enterprises (MSMEs). Yet, we wanted to avoid the trappings of so many corporate 'innovation theatres' that have consumed finite resources – and, more importantly, enterprise hope – while delivering limited impact. The following is an account of our eXellerator lab journey, the strengths of the Bank that we drew on, and the lessons we learned along the way.

The jury is still out in terms of our impact on the transformation of Standard Chartered Bank. Based on our approach of enabling the Bank to embrace change and new mindsets; adopting fintechs as strategic partners for change; challenging and redefining what good operating and business models look like; and changing the perception of clients, albeit a relatively small group now, to see us as more than just a trusted bank but equal partners to test and build new technology, platforms and business ventures that tap into new opportunities. Overall, I think we have a good shot at enabling real change in the Bank.

EMBRACING CHANGE

At the beginning, predating SC Ventures, was the eXellerator Lab at Standard Chartered Bank.

It was a Sunday in 2017 when the then Chief Data and Innovation Officer (CDO) called to ask if I would consider running the eXellerator, the precursor to SC Ventures, in addition to my role as the Head of Data and Analytics Enablement. The eXellerator was 12-18 months old at the time and had experienced some management challenges. It took me two minutes to accept.

Over my 18 years in Standard Chartered Bank, I had worked across seven different regional and global roles (three of which I had created), while undergoing acquisitions and integrations, launching and relaunching our global client strategy, and offshoring interests to reduce running costs, all while surviving the global financial crisis. This experience has taught me something unique about change within the Bank: if you have your heart in the right place, the right capabilities and a bold plan, someone will back you up to effect meaningful change.

> *"If you have your heart in the right place, the right capabilities, and a bold plan, someone will back you up to effect meaningful change."*

Embracing change and empowering the change agents were always in the DNA of this bank, turning adversity, like a galvanising force, into an opportunity.

BUT WHAT WAS DIFFERENT THIS TIME?

On the first day, conversations with the eXellerator team started with them wondering why I had been tasked with leading them. I was committed to helping the team succeed by connecting them to sponsors in the Bank, establishing social contracts, setting 'professional irreverence' as a shared work ethic, ensuring that everyone was empowered to challenge, and redefining what *good* looks like from the outside. The first clear difference was that hierarchy and years of service meant little to those who were anxious to land the impactful punches of change.

> *"Hierarchy and years of service meant very little to those who were anxious to land the impactful punches of change."*

The pace of change was much faster, so traditional three-year programmes were out, and iterative, agile, swift and nimble test-and-learn systems were in. Technology and data accessibility changed the rules and pace of the game. We could test and train models using a much wider and more diverse set of data.

Our competitors were also different: we were not looking over our shoulders at other banks to see who would break into a canter first. Instead, it was felt that 'the fintechs would have the banks for lunch'. The scale and pace of these new competitors were truly inspiring – two examples of which are engraved on my memory:

- The development of a mobile app with biometric authentication that could use a voice application process for loans while simultaneously scanning changes in facial expressions for potential fraud. This meant that money from successful loan applications could transfer within six minutes of approval.

- Technology that allows the digital images of damaged motor vehicles to be sent to a marketplace of parts distributors and garages. These would be able to return quotes, with an offer and acceptance completed within minutes, to process motor insurance claims.

Wow! The bankers watching the demonstrations were definitely feeling some pressure.

The change partners were also different. In place of vendors who delivered the bank's defined requirements, we were meeting fintechs who spoke about their purpose and vision. Some of the founders had left banking with clear convictions that there was a need for a different way to work, make decisions, to use the vast amount of data and new technology available to accelerate change. Some did not know the banking industry and brought with them the humility to learn about it, while displaying a strong conviction that their products could revolutionise our operating models.

LEARNING TO DANCE

First, bankers needed to accept partnerships with fintechs without suggestions around how the legacy mindset, technology and operating models were not the right fit. It also needed different attitudes towards the way partnerships were forged. In fact, it was crucial to have some clear problem statements.

Some of the key success factors we identified were: 1) strong business stakeholder sponsorship; and 2) committed subject-matter experts who could frame clear problem statements with us. They would define their minimum success criteria, work with the fintechs through proof of concept (POC), and pursue what was possible in automating/digitising existing processes and also in fundamentally redesigning them.

The clincher, however, was gaining commitment from Chief Information Officers (CIOs), Chief Technology Officers (CTOs) and Chief Operating Officers (COOs) to launch successful POCs into production and scale them across our network of up to 60 markets. For many of the artificial intelligence (AI) based solutions, doing the hard yards and gaining support from the business and Chief Data Officer (CDO) teams to create a safe environment, engineer the right data set to train the models, and validate the model integrity for better decisions and predictions, was richly rewarding.

Ultimately, what fintechs truly seek are partners who are willing to work with them to test their solutions, challenge and sharpen

The eXellerator: Old Meets New 35

their value propositions, and (where they have proven their solutions and capabilities) implement and scale their products across multiple markets.

In the first year, we found new truths. First, most of the fintechs we spoke to and worked with, were not out to 'eat our lunches'. Instead, they offered some truly new and insightful ways of addressing and solving many of banking's legacy problems. Second, many of them were like the best and brightest teenagers (with respect) in our families: given the right nurturing and empowerment, they have the potential to grow into truly bright stars, venturing far across multiple clients, banks and industries, surpassing our expectations. Third, when there was an alignment of purpose between these new partners and the Bank, these relationships could flourish to the benefit of the Bank, by changing our idea of what good banking looks like, and by collectively making this fintech ecosystem scalable and sustainable.

Critically, the fintech relationship and role in the transformation of banking can only thrive if banks and financial institutions recognise them as partners and a source of rich talents, that can challenge us to redesign and reimagine banking services. The worst-case scenario would be to treat them as small vendors from whom the big boys can squeeze out every good idea and intellectual property (IP) to replicate and justify their IT departments.

Working with fintechs also has unintended consequences. It was only a few years ago that onboarding a fintech was nigh on impossible. Our fintech team consciously partnered with teams from vendor management, technology risk assessment, cloud engineering, and legal, to define what a risk differentiated POC framework might look like. The challenge was to be able to launch a low-risk, synthetic data-based POC in two weeks. When we finally launched this for two POCs, it was game-changing and welcome news to many of our fintech partners. Organisationally, it created a common purpose and a belief that we could create a risk-based approach to governance and compliance that would accelerate fintech exploration and refresh the technology within the Bank. In a (small) way, it helped the eXellerator to build a more mature relationship with the main Bank's risk and governance function.

Two years on, as we found our value proposition for fintechs, we began to ask real questions about the scalability of our engagement model. How many POCs could we run in a year? How quickly could we scale them? How do we break through the old mindset of just automating and digitising parts of a badly designed legacy process? Could we start combining these different capabilities to redesign an operating model? Or, better still, redesign banking and make our value proposition far more compelling and inclusive? Like many corporate innovation labs, we only had the mandate to explore, test and deploy new technology as a separate unit, so the eXellerator construct could not answer these questions.

CLIENT ENGAGEMENTS: FROM 'INNOVATION TOURISM' TO PROPER CO-CREATION

Clients are the lifeline of our business. Traditionally, with the best of intentions, banks invest significantly to design ever better products and services, than those offered by their competitors. Then they provide these to their clients. Fintechs were disrupting this narrative, and the same was true for many of our clients and markets. Significant clients of ours had seen their market capitalisation deteriorate significantly as a result of the emergence of e-commerce platform companies. At the same time, new technology was promising to make international businesses far more transparent, cost-efficient and accessible to a larger number of organisations.

So, client interest in our eXellerator lab naturally began to emerge. Admittedly, there was often a measure of scepticism for 'real change' coming from a bank, which they wanted to validate. It was also a 'hedge' ahead of granting us a new mandate, where they wanted to make sure that we would remain a viable partner for the medium to long term. For the most part, though, I remained unconvinced that they knew what outcome they really wanted from these 'first dates', where we wooed them with ideas, workshops, and demonstrations of our smart prototypes, usually over evening drinks and feel-good conversations. As good as those sessions were, there was rarely a 'second date' to follow through on the ideas we had discussed.

The eXellerator: Old Meets New   37

With the creation of SC Ventures and a broader mandate across fintechs, investments and new ventures, we started thinking of the eXellerator in a completely different way: specifically, in the context of our proposition for clients.

We began to ask some important questions:

- What was top of mind for our clients, either facing disruption or seizing opportunities?
- What can we offer to help them accelerate and meet their needs?
- What new possibilities could we collectively create for both of us if we combined our capabilities, network reach and IP?

The question was how to convert the goodwill and genuine interest we generated on our 'first dates' into work. In the first instance, this meant following up on one or more of the ideas we had discussed, perhaps in the form of a more structured workshop. Such interaction would then typically yield a new product or service that was specifically designed to address our client's needs. Over time, some of these solutions could even evolve into venture ideas in their own right, under the assumption that if we innovatively solved one client's problem, others may well have the same problem and we could commercialise the solution more broadly, possibly co-operating with X who had identified the problem in the first place.

We went as far as defining the 'three stages' of client engagement: 1) 'innovation tourism', which has a negative or cynical connotation, but we made it clear to ourselves that it was absolutely 'part of the job' to make ourselves available for any such interactions with any meaningful client of the Bank; 2) co-creation workshops; and 3) venturing together.

As we pivoted our 'innovation tourism' conversations to what clients needed and to where our combined comparative advantage was, we created a pipeline and significantly increased the number of follow-throughs, 'deep dive workshops', exploratory prototyping and co-creation initiatives in the second category. And, over time, some of the venture ideas in the third category started to emerge.

Most significantly, these clients now see Standard Chartered as being more than a bank. They see us as a technology builder – a strategic venture partner with whom they can create and test new revenue opportunities.

TAKEAWAYS

- With any new partnership, strong business stakeholder sponsorship and committed subject-matter experts who could frame clear problem statements are key elements for success.

- We needed to move clients from 'innovation tourism' to potential investors or clients; offer more structured, detailed workshops to follow up on initial conversations.

6

TASCONNECT: THE OPERATING SYSTEM OF TRADE

Gautam Jain[a] and Apurv Suri[b]

[a]Operating Member
[b]Member, Client Engagement Lead

TASConnect is a bank-agnostic, fully customizable supply chain finance platform for large institutions, providing automation, visibility and control to create opportunities in their value chains.

"We had the ability to validate not just the problem statements at hand, but every step of the creation of the platform."

TASConnect in a nutshell: TASConnect is a SaaS (Software as a service) working capital solution platform, which brings together an organisation's supply chain ecosystem, including their suppliers and banks, on a single platform. This enables organisations to have an end-to-end view of their supply chain through a single window.

The tie-up: We were approached by the relationship team of one of our key corporate clients, who were exploring how to make their large supply chain more efficient, by digitising and automating its financing aspects. They wanted to deploy this for their treasury and had sent their proposal to multiple banks and tech vendors and were in the middle of shortlisting.

THE LITMUS TEST FOR TASCONNECT

The SC Ventures team was forming our client engagement 2.0 strategy when the first TASConnect conversation started. We were asking: how can we bring innovation to our clients in a way that has not been done before? And how can we bring innovation that offers meaningful partnership and opportunities for collective growth in the cross-section of the client's industry and ours? While we were excited to bring our proposition forward to real clients, we had some doubts about whether clients would relate to it and take meaningful next steps to work together. This developing opportunity saw our doubts quickly shift to a clear focus and became a litmus test as to whether we could truly realise the potential of joint venturing with our clients.

The early stages of the engagement gave us insights that helped form our thinking beyond TASConnect. We realised the potential value of the whole client engagement side of our platform, where we could partner with relationship teams to equip them with tools and techniques to offer to their clients. We were confident that what we could offer, had the power to change our clients' perception of SC Ventures from 'service providers' to partners and thought leaders, in a world where most of our client industries were going through some form of disruption. We balanced this confidence with the short-term and deal-led lens that sales and relationship teams typically adopt, with the outstanding questions being: How do I incentivise and inspire? How do I get the teams outside of SC Ventures that 'manage' the client relationship to recognise this USP? We decided to lead by example and to build credibility, through executing the deal and then communicating this well.

WHO SAID THAT CONVINCING A CLIENT IS EASY?

Any person who has sat in a sales role will relate to the above question. Now, imagine a situation where not only are you defining a strategy for creating a joint venture on one side, but you are also – in some instances – creating a high-stakes game with an important client of the Bank. Our clients are more familiar with dealing with us on more traditional and core banking products and services; and yet, while the nature of our interaction with them on ventures is decidedly new and different, our client's expectations around structure, guidance and results remain the same.

The client had approached us with a proposed approach and therefore *convincing* them of our venture-building capabilities, and that we were solving this problem for a wider ecosystem, became key in the early stages. It was comforting that there was immense support for solving the wider ecosystem on both sides. Against this backdrop, the client problems were the driver that helped us collaborate with the unified goal of building a unique value proposition – bringing it to the market with our collective brands and expertise, to create an offering that has been built *by* practitioners *for* practitioners.

At the same time, something interesting was transpiring in the core working team. There was a transformation in dialogue and mannerisms. We were transitioning from a 'vendor' type of discussion, to one where there was an open dialogue inclusive of friendly, yet edgy, challenges about what this platform could do. The candour and transparency between the team members meant we could have open discussions about what we were solving *for* (the client versus the wider ecosystem) and where we could take the platform together as partners.

TRUST, TRUST, TRUST ...

At some point during any venture's journey, the question arises: What differentiates you? We asked that question to the client in the first instance. Why not use one of the many third-party platforms that exist in this space? Why build something of your own?

Their response was as follows:

- **Trust:** A lack of *trust* was a big factor when looking at third-party fintechs and platforms. There was a specific instance where the client had almost finalised a proof of concept (POC) with a competitor of TASConnect, only to drop it because of operational challenges. This was a small point in the whole scheme of things, but it amplified the risks that come with adopting new platforms.

- **Integration:** Typically, as a treasurer, you may not have as much interaction with the IT department of your organisation. Based on our initial research into the integration hypothesis, a client would require anywhere from 8 to 11 separate integrations with platforms to get an end-to-end view of their supply chain financing programmes.

- **Fragmentation:** Connected to the above point on integration, the market is – and continues to be – very fragmented and saturated in its offering. It currently consists of specialised providers servicing niches in the end-to-end supply chain journey. This is split into two separate 'legs' – procurement and financing – followed by further steps around integration that both procurement and financing take.

The beauty of this co-creation was that we could validate not just the problem statements at hand, but every step of the creation of the platform. Except for the client usability versus wider ecosystem dilemma, this was one of the most powerful impacts of co-creating with an institutional user of the envisaged solution.

MINIMUM VIABLE 'PRODUCT'?

Challenge: What is the minimum viable value that we can take to market? First, we are bringing trust in the form of this market-first partnership. The trust of a bank can ensure that bank-grade controls, compliance, risk and governance are adhered to. And the trust that the tech products our partner brings through its day-to-day business are reliable. Second, the platform will be an operating system. By plugging into the corporate's enterprise resource planning (ERP) systems, it will be able to connect to any specialised providers based on client demand and the client's relationship banks. Finally, TASConnect will offer its core capabilities of accounts receivable and accounts payable, with the ability to customise and digitise the workflow, which clients will typically access through separate data instances of the platform.

Beyond the minimum viable value, the platform will use the data it has accessed to provide further value-added services.

These include anonymised ratings of suppliers who are serving the same anchors and contextualised behavioural and repayment patterns to enable anchors to understand their supplier risk and focus areas in their supply chains. Sticking to our promise of delivering value to both sides of the equation, we are also working with fintechs to provide suppliers with industry payment term benchmarks and a script that will enable them to renegotiate payment terms with their anchors, so they can have a more efficient working capital structure.

While it is still early days, TASConnect has the foundations in place and the flexibility to respond to client and market demands as well as ongoing trends in the trade finance space.

TIME AND ACCOUNTABILITY

A further key aspect we have reflected on during this journey, has been the time to market and the accountability we maintain as partners towards each other. We had critical deadlines to meet at the start of the project, intensified by the COVID environment, which could have led to perpetual brainstorming fatigue, without any actionable deadlines. However, through this journey, we held each other accountable, and that dynamic of a client – bank relationship played in our favour: in one way, shape or form, we were sticking to being client-centric and delivering value to a key client of the Bank, albeit as partners rather than service providers.

TAKEAWAYS

- Flexibility is key when it comes to partnering with a corporate – you cannot force structure or process when co-creating.

- When co-creating, ensuring the proposition is beyond a single use case (not just solving for one client at a time) is critical in the roadmap of a venture.

- When partnering with a client, a clear vision is imperative to the success and outcome of a venture.

7

THE eXELLERATOR: NEW MEETS OLD

Jen McAuliffe

Previous Member, Intrapreneurship Lead

"The eXellerator space is purposefully designed to support co-design, collaboration and co-location."

Having helped set up the innovation lab for a large Australian bank, I was hired to help Standard Chartered Bank do the same. In my new role, our purpose was clear: we were not there to innovate *for* the Bank, nor were we the only innovation group trying to do things better. Rather, our role was to enable innovation through providing practical hands-on experience, education and connection.

CREATING A MULTIDISCIPLINARY TEAM

We started the journey by creating our lab – 'eXellerator' – which consisted of a handful of entrepreneurs-in-residence: several innovation coaches, a technologist, a fintech engagement expert and a communications manager. Experience in banking and finance at a large corporation, while helpful, was not essential for joining our design-led team. We sought candidates who had a multidisciplinary background across human-centred design and 'Lean or Agile' practices, but who were not purists in any one of these areas. It was key to have the mindset and character to challenge pre-conceived ideas, draw out the real problem, and encourage conversations and research with customers.

LAUNCHING THE FIRST EXELLERATOR

There are some clichés in the innovation lab space, and ours was no different. We started out making the physical space look different from the corporate office – complete with beanbags and quirky names that no one could spell. While it might seem trivial, it was important to portray a different way of thinking and working, and to facilitate those ways in an appropriately inspiring work area.

BUILDING A CREATIVE SPACE

When setting up the space, the team came in over the weekend to remove desk dividers and reposition the furniture, as were eager to get started. This was just one example of the speed at which we wanted to operate, in order to get things moving.

Our early descriptions of the eXellerator and its purpose were as follows:

- The eXellerator is primarily an accelerator for business problems, where we use a fundamentally different approach to 'get stuff done' and deliver capability, typically in the form of some kind of prototype or test-and-learn scenario. (To differentiate ourselves from standard project work, we referred to our work on each business problem as an 'initiative'. Much of what we were helping teams to do was pre-project work: framing the problem, conducting customer research, and building prototypes – and therefore, in many cases, helping to build a business case.)

- The eXellerator space is purposefully designed to support co-design, collaboration and co-location. We encourage teams to sit together when looking at their business problem or opportunity, and to 'work-out-loud' which means lots of visuals, whiteboards and Post-It notes. Teams participate in daily stand-ups and regular showcases of their work. They could demonstrate their working solutions and ideas to senior sponsors, stakeholders and even customers. It also promotes feedback and conversations with other teams working in the eXellerator.

Initially, it was difficult to convince our business stakeholders on the value of getting a team of people together to collaborate on a problem for two or three days, or longer. Some of them were used to different ways of working, which involved a broader group of stakeholders and layered decision-making processes. We had to adjust our approach and run workshops and sessions lasting two to three hours. Yet, once they started to see the outputs, the first participants to do this came back again and again, and for longer and longer sessions.

We found like-minded people across the Bank and began to build our arsenal of success cases. They included:

- Achieving material savings on consultancy fees as a result of a three-day workshop for a team so they could understand and frame a problem they were trying to solve.

- Researching, prototyping and testing a banking product for a large corporation and investment bank client that addressed the majority of their key pain points. This translated into material wallet share for that part of the business.

- Helping teams in the Transaction Banking division come up with, and progress ideas for their own growth challenges.

- Building connections and shared understanding between product teams and clients, by conducting workshops and sessions with industry experts to feed future strategies.

The challenge was measuring success in terms of 'service' to the business. If the business problem was to cut costs, we contributed to that success by helping to find solutions. If it was about better engagement with customers to build a 'stickier' relationship and increase wallet share, our work contributed to that, too. But it was not easy to measure those successes once the initiative had been absorbed back into business-as-usual. Consequently, the Bank evolved its innovation scorecard for our contributions.

FROM ONE TO MORE

In 2016, we participated in the Monetary Authority of Singapore's first ever Singapore Fintech Festival. From this, we launched a month of innovation events. Participation in the festival required us to open the eXellerator to the public.

We had to be creative about what we would showcase. To that end, we came up with a mini-trade show. We put together various stands demonstrating the kinds of technology that our businesses were exploring – 3D printing, virtual and augmented reality, and blockchain. We even built a blockchain machine to help businesses visualise how a distributed ledger works (this came on the road with us many times!). We also invited businesses and partners to showcase their own innovation efforts and proofs of concept (POCs).

Additionally, we used the festival as an opportunity to open up the eXellerator to staff as well as the public. This created a buzz and awareness, but there were still plenty of areas unaware of our existence across the Bank. Therefore, our next aim was to better support our teams across the globe.

Following our involvement in the Singapore Fintech Festival, we hit the road and held a week-long event in Hong Kong in 2016. A large space was subsequently earmarked for a new eXellerator there, which was to be run by WeWork and also act as a common staff area.

Over the next couple of years, we set up an eXellerator presence in additional locations, including London, Nairobi and Shanghai. Most of these new locations were preceded by a pop-up innovation event or roadshow. Here, we would put together a week or so of events, training, showcases and workshops. This helped gather support from key stakeholders – who would become the lab's

The eXellerator: New Meets Old

49

future 'customers' – and in some cases also helped us secure physical space and co-funding.

Over the past five years, our Fintech Festival 'open house' has grown from that initial demonstration of new technologies to a true showcase of our work on case studies and with fintech partners; work that is being used and applied across the Bank today. We maintained the trade show format and expanded it to include panel discussions and presentations. Some of those initial fintech firms are now key partners of the Bank and part of the SC Ventures investment portfolio.

As our team and the demand for our services grew, we regularly contemplated our purpose, vision and mission. It always came back to helping to solve business problems, building a culture of innovation, and exploring new technologies. We provided a place for teams to explore technologies and run POCs within their business areas.

Initially, there was a fear that our eXellerator brand would be lost. In the process of rebranding, we dropped our beloved hashtag (#makeshifthappen), lost our e-signatures, and our T-shirts now said 'SC Ventures'. But that disruption of ourselves has given us a broader reach with stakeholders and more credibility as a team. It is almost as if our eXellerator has grown up!

> *"... disruption of ourselves has given us a broader reach with stakeholders and more credibility as a team. It's almost as if our eXellerator has grown up!"*

With the evolution of SC Ventures, the eXellerator brand became part of something much bigger. In addition to the internal business focus that we already had, we were now helping to build and create business model innovation (ideas that could spin off into true *ventures*). It could also provide the Bank with an investment fund focused purely on finding technology and fintech companies that would benefit us, as a whole. Another bonus was that the banking team brought an innovation platform with them, that we were able to launch globally alongside our Intrapreneurs Programme. This was a way the Bank could connect with us and truly be a part of the innovation community.

TAKEAWAYS

- Situate your lab close to clients and stakeholders if you want them to visit for demonstrations and co-creation.

- Ensure your physical space is flexible and fit for purpose (which may change over time).

- Be wary of disrupting a project that is already in flight. People do not like to be challenged on whether they are solving the right problem, if they are already six months into the journey.

- Recognise that language is important. An *idea*, an *initiative*, a *project*, a *problem* and a *solution* are all different things.

8

BUILDING THE SC VENTURES FINTECH BRIDGE

Harald Eltvedt[a] and Simran Gill[b]

[a]*Operating Member*
[b]*Member*

"Startups needed to engage with decision makers for their key challenges, from demonstrating their capabilities to pitching their solutions and getting the investment they needed to grow. We needed to design an ecosystem that sticks the community of fintechs, corporate clients, and the Bank together."

The ambition to build a large community of startups had come at the very beginning of SC Ventures. We needed to have a sizeable impact in the fintech ecosystem, broaden our research from the start, and have the startups organised in a marketplace for them to be identified by the Bank and our partners.

SC Ventures' FinTech Bridge started in 2018, when we set up a competition to enrol startups on a project for Group Retail Banking, and eventually shortlisted only two winners. That approach was difficult to scale and hardly sustainable, as solutions already existed in the market, in the form of the myriads of accelerator programmes that were bringing connections to startups.

We needed to be more engaging for startups so that our projects could operate within a shorter time frame, at a global scale, and at a lower cost. The design of our FinTech Bridge was on its way to starting a virtuous circle that would generate fintechs to sign up, create visibility of our ecosystem of ventures and engagement with the Bank.

APPEALING AND SIMPLE

By creating their profile on the platform, fintechs can describe their solution and access either business challenges to solve for, or pitch for investment in a direct, short journey. Additionally, the platform gives them much more than answering their first expectations: it makes them active members of a vibrant network. It is about bringing together a whole community of fintechs, giving them direct access to one another, so they can exchange and grow their business; it is about getting access to the challenges that the Bank shares with them, to address a concrete issue, and offering their solution to solve it.

For the Bank, we built a library of solutions, along with the various registered profiles: from the start, the reaction from fintechs was positive, and in less than a year we had enrolled more than 500.

NOT A STRAIGHT ROAD

Building the platform was only the beginning of the journey. Our first experience taught us how critically important it is to choose the right development and implementation team. We created the best recipe: an agile team of developers working closely with the implementation team in sprints, and not attempting to cut corners on the user experience, user interface, platform architecture, coding quality or security standards. This platform wanted to offer a differentiated value proposition, so it had to show a strong commitment to startups and treat them in the same way we do with our corporate clients – ideally, via our relationship managers.

Unlike the eXellerator lab, which applied an internal perspective – how to make the Bank embrace innovation and human-centred design (HCD) – we wanted to look at it through a different lens, that of the startups and their priority: providing an ecosystem where they could pitch their solution to get new use cases wherever they can be applied and find the direct path to the right people.

Most of the time, startups follow the same steps: 1) understand the organisation; 2) get contacts; 3) build connections, and 4) pitch their solution. This alone could take weeks or months. One of the key issues startups consistently reported was that corporations did not have the right mindset or expertise to understand them, leading to difficulty in obtaining buy-in. This led to more people being involved in the discussion, further extending the process.

Key learnings from our engagement with the community that brought us to design the SC Ventures FinTech Bridge platform were:

- The need for a global ecosystem that connects startups to the Bank and its corporate stakeholders.

- Faster engagement for fintechs, at a global scale and lower cost.

- Linking the right people to the startups and facilitating the connection.

- Solving bona fide business challenges with technology (as opposed to 'technology solutions looking for a problem')

DESIGNING AND BUILDING THE RIGHT ECOSYSTEM

Because the separation of internal and external needs overlapped, we decided to adapt our existing innovation tool, SC Innovate across the entire Bank, and expand it to external use. On SC Innovate, employees would answer problem statements with their own ideas.

With the new Fintech Bridge, it was a matter of turning that tool into producing more practical answers and getting the external startup community to respond as well.

We decided to build the platform from scratch, working in sprints, with the aim of releasing a first Minimum Viable Product (MVP) within five months. It would work towards first:

Releasing a platform with key features,

- which would be adjusted and improved over time,
- based on user feedback.

As of June 2024, SC Ventures had engaged with more than 25,000 employees and enrolled over 3,000 fintechs on the FinTech Bridge platform.

ADOPTION FROM FINTECHS AND THE BANK

Fintechs could now create their own profiles, containing key information and content for the Bank and its corporate clients, to better assess their proposition.

For the Bank, the platform enabled staff and corporate stakeholders to access the full library of registered startup profiles. Once they registered their preferences, staff and stakeholders would receive notifications whenever a new fintech that matched their interests joined the community.

There were three main reasons that enabled early adoption by fintechs: 1) the platform's value proposition had been built with them; 2) the platform was launched at Money2020, an event with high startup participation; and 3) the platform had gotten good ongoing media coverage.

However, the reaction from internal stakeholders was less warm at first: they needed to be convinced to at least try to use the platform. To achieve that, it was important to address some of their objections.

One of their initial objections was to share problem statements with the market and, by extension, with their competitors. Our answers were that we would likely find useful solutions by looking externally, and not just internally, but never share genuinely confidential information.

Another adoption challenge was being the first to use the platform and finding a champion that would provide us with the initial use case. We were able to do so with a business of the bank that wanted help on a challenge. Serving them well was a great opportunity to gain ground inside the Bank. This first challenge was followed by others, totalling eight challenges within three months, which cemented our reputation, and initiated real use within the Bank.

The first release of SC Ventures FinTech Bridge had set up good foundations: connected startups to our internal business stakeholders (decision makers) with an objective to generate new business opportunities for the startups within the shortest possible time.

FROM MVP TO FINTECH BRIDGE 3.0

Our first year of activity had been spent on improving the platform's performance and getting use cases from the business.

In parallel, we launched a new design plan, with the following objectives:

- Build on the target audience and their needs.
- Identify improvements in terms of user experience.
- Find opportunities to open up the ecosystem for collaboration and networking.
- Adapt to Web 3.0 capabilities.

A sample of corporate clients, bank employees, accelerators and investors were interviewed to further identify additional needs and confirm our assumptions for the new platform.

MOVING FROM PLATFORM TO 'FINTECH ENGAGEMENT'

The platform is no longer simply an ecosystem for connecting people; it is about bridging communities with common interests and ways of working (or the desire to change their ways of working). Boundaries no longer exist between internal and external ecosystems. Members (and not just users) can connect people, projects, problems, ideas, solutions, and content. The Bank has become a key enabler for these communities.

Engaging with fintechs is a two-way street. The evolution of the FinTech Bridge has provided a strong platform for our community to grow and interact. We are now taking a forward-looking view of the Fintech Engagement activities by increasing our partnerships with Associations, Regulators, and venture capitalists (VCs) across our footprint and building deeper networks within the ecosystem. To compliment this, we further look to increase participation within markets where there is the increasing emergence of modern technologies, capabilities, and investments (in some cases, also extending beyond our footprint). This does not only look to complement our themes but also helps shape SC Ventures by being at forefront of future trends and themes.

Bringing this together equips our platform to be well positioned in solving problem statements and stronger community engagement – ultimately driving more outcomes through proof of concepts (POCs) and investments through our fund. At the time of writing this, we are continuously looking to expand our existing capabilities through adding scouting services, which adds an extra dimension of external validation and enablement to our partners (for their proprietary purposes).

TAKEAWAYS

- Having as open an ecosystem as possible.
- Growing the Bank's value proposition to the fintech ecosystem.
- Treating startups in the same way we do corporate clients by being appealing, direct and simple.
- Giving the Bank a powerful library of solutions to answer their needs and those of their corporate clients.
- Building from an existing tool, while adapting it to external, allowed gaining time and enhancing adoption.

9

CORPORATE VENTURE CAPITAL INVESTMENT: TOO CLOSE OR TOO FAR – RARELY JUST RIGHT

Alex Manson

CEO, SC Ventures

"We meant to set up a different effort that would ... cement partnerships where we genuinely helped start-ups grow and scale, at the same time as they helped us to transform our bank."

Corporate venture capital (CVC) typically disappoints, when it does not just fail outright. This is because it is either so close to the corporate that it is doomed to make mistakes and behave in a clunky fashion, or because it is so distant that the corporate gets little out of it and loses interest.

Most ominously, before they can even lead to the outcomes described above, both types of CVC set-ups have a terrible and immediate secondary effect: they cannibalise resources – in this case, mostly investment dollars – that could have been deployed by the corporate towards genuine innovation.

Learning from this, we wanted to do something different and avoid the traps of either of the above extremes. We certainly did not want to act at the expense of a true and more holistic innovation effort in and around the Bank. We wanted a different model that would serve a purpose: to cement partnerships where we genuinely helped startups grow and scale, at the same time as they helped us to transform our bank. (Financial returns requirements were seen as an operating constraint, not as a purpose.) So, we designed governance for our fund dedicated to that purpose and started operating it in, what outsiders said, was record time.

TOO CLOSE

CVC is sometimes so strategic that it is completely integrated into the corporation that sponsors it – living on the balance sheet, controlled by the corporation, and obeying its decision-making and due diligence processes.

'Strategic' here means that investment executives are investing in what they – or the firm – believe are capabilities of strategic relevance, which is defined by their views of the moment. These may have financial returns as an objective, but the returns of investments may bring other benefits.

The way this type of CVC effort first disappoints, is that its governance is unwieldy; being completely integrated with the corporation means being subject to corporation-led governance.

Startups and venture capitalists (VCs) leading a funding round might at times find themselves negotiating at length on issues unusual for the VC market. (This may be due to internal procedures or, at times, legitimate regulatory requirements.) The startups/VCs then make their way to an investment committee, only to find that additional changes to the process and the terms of the deal are requested, or the deal is simply turned down.

This is the main reason why, in the initial days of corporates 'venturing' into the investment space, many professional VCs swore to avoid 'strategic investors'. This meant the best deals were quickly snapped up by professional investors and not shared with CVC ones, while the more difficult or less-compelling transactions were brought to such CVCs, affecting their returns.

Finally, 'strategic' is an overarching objective that can be used to justify lots of poor decisions, especially when it is vaguely defined. The strategic benefits of an investment may not always be immediately quantifiable but should ultimately be tangible. Many CVCs failed to realise such benefits, for example, because they invested in great capabilities or ideas that the corporation ended up never using at all.

TOO FAR

At the opposite extreme, the CVC effort is truly separate and distinct from the corporation that sponsors it, constituting a separate legal entity with separate governance, including a professional investment committee. This committee is fit for purpose in the context of the VC market, meaning that decision-making happens in the time frame of a VC round, that standard term sheets are acceptable, and that these CVC professionals deal with their VC counterparts like peers that speak the same language. Some corporations learnt from the failure of the first model and ended up later segregating their investment efforts (or 'spinning them out') to achieve the second model.

Such an effort could well be very successful in financial terms. This type of CVC is often respected in the industry as a valuable partner to have and is less likely to make costly 'strategic' mistakes, as it is driven by strict financial returns criteria. However, it has typically disappointed its backers differently: it is so well segregated from the mothership that one wonders how the mothership benefits from it at all. Pipeline selection is generally claimed to be made in collaboration with the corporation, but the level of integration is so remote that the CVC effort often ends up with a portfolio that has only limited correlation with any actual or future use by the corporation. Executives, not being in an 'ownership' position, feel less compelled to work with portfolio companies, other than when the stars are aligned. This could be the difference between investments that scale internally and those that do not.

Such efforts, therefore, while potentially profitable in their own right, are also often too small to matter in the context of the scale of the corporation backing them. They take too long to bring both financial and strategic benefits, leading to the final nail in the coffin: the CVC gets interrupted early, or is subject to the whims of the corporate environment (be they budgetary constraints, change in management, or loss of interest). This last point is especially critical, as it takes several years of consistency and commitment to yield both financial and strategic benefits, and also to establish a reputation in the investment market as a reliable partner.

JUST NEVER RIGHT, UNLESS ...

It is often those same companies that set up a US$100 million dollars investment fund that struggles to find US$100,000 for a fintech proof of concept (POC). However, management can argue that they are committed to innovation since they dedicated the resources to invest in it; the US$100 million dollars may simply represent lip service towards innovation efforts. Learning from this, we wanted to do something different, avoiding the traps of either of the extremes described above, and certainly not acting at the expense of a true and more holistic innovation effort in and around the Bank.

It was also clear that we needed to avoid the cultural clashes posed by stark differences in compensation systems, such as the Ventures group being incentivised by a 'carried interest' while others were not. However, we also needed to avoid the traps of 'strategic investments' and to maintain a tight financial discipline, while the overall effort still had to be transformational for the Bank.

So, we designed a very specific set-up (after multiple iterations of test, fail and adjust). The governance went like this: we engaged three external advisors on our investment committee, which also has three Bank representatives. Both blocks vote independently. For investment decisions, it then takes two to agree and one to disagree. Importantly, the carry goes to the advisors, so that they are genuinely incentivised to achieve VC-like financial returns.

In other words: we as a bank understand the use case, the technology or capability and how to apply it. We also get to know the management teams of the company and test their implementation

Corporate Venture Capital Investment

and ability to support the venture over time. If successful, we can become a very credible reference for these companies (and have done that over time – it is part of the deal). On the other end, external advisors bring a view of the market, with a good understanding of trends, dynamics and alternative offerings. Importantly, they ensure that we buy at the right price – and sell at the right time – as we will see in the following chapters.

TAKEAWAYS

- We had to balance how close the corporation was to the venture with the support we needed from the Bank.

- There are benefits to working in this way even when we know that corporate-backed ventures will often fail.

- We took time to look at what cultural clashes may occur and acted to reduce these through how we rewarded the team.

10

THE BIRTH OF JARVIS

Gautam Jain

Operating Member

"The founding team did a lot of early thinking around what success would look like for the fund."

In 2016 we came across Ripple, a small startup based out of the US West Coast. The more we worked with them, the more we were impressed by their thinking and people, and consequently ended up investing in them. This early and successful investment in a blockchain firm set the foundation of the corporate investment fund for the Bank, to take minority stakes in fintech companies that it uses in its product and service suite. Our vision was to help the Bank stay ahead of the curve in technological innovation, and to act as a catalyst in our goal to 'rewire the DNA' of the Bank. At the same time, this goal could not succeed unless we placed a greater emphasis on financial returns, and in designing our investment fund. We needed to straddle both goals.

When started thinking about the setup of the fund, the name that was given to the project was 'Jarvis', a reference to the smart computer in *Iron Man*. (The name is short for 'Just A Rather Very Intelligent System', which was exactly what we were looking for.)

At the outset, the Jarvis founding team grappled with a multitude of existential questions, including:

- What is the objective of investing through the fund? Is it strategic benefits, pure financial returns, or both?

- How do we set this up for success? Do we outsource the investment process to external advisors, or manage it closely within the business?

- What would success look like in the next five to ten years?

They discussed and iterated on the operating model with various stakeholders and did a lot of early thinking around what success would look like for the fund – in terms of both quantitative parameters (investments made, returns achieved) and qualitative ones (external brand-building, impact on the Bank's performance). While this might seem like 'over-engineering' at an early stage, when there are a lot of unknowns, and no one can predict the trajectory going forward, it helped to buy into a shared vision of success.

During this thinking, we also took a few key decisions. We decided to appoint independent advisors to the investment committee to bring in industry expertise in the field of fintech investing, and to provide a degree of independence to both our investment and divestment decisions. We also took the decision that fund members would be compensated through the Bank's normal evaluation process, and that their compensation would not be linked to fund performance in the form of carried interest. Additionally, we decided to appoint an independent third party as fund administrators, as well as an independent valuation advisory firm. We wanted to bring in as much external expertise as possible, while balancing the interests of the Bank, and our team.

NAVIGATING THE CORPORATE PROCESS

We had a unique challenge: how to define a process for investing (and divesting), including the terms of reference for the investment committee, to achieve the following:

The Birth of Jarvis   65

- Be fast and nimble.

- Mitigate risk.

- Keep stakeholders involved and happy.

While we were unsure what the process should look like, we recognised that we operate in the Bank's ecosystem – which meant there are processes and layers already in existence, and therefore steps the Bank would expect us to take when looking to invest. One of the processes was based on how the Bank manages large acquisitions and divestments. Speed was important, balanced with the right process for decision-making. Fintech rounds normally close in eight to ten weeks, and it is unlikely that investors would wait longer than that for our process. The Bank's processes require multiple layers of sign-off (usually, a corporate function), which ultimately could have slowed us down. As an outcome, we worked with the Bank in designing leaner processes to support our activity. Ultimately, with the support of many teams like Group Corporate Development, we launched a 'light' version of the existing process, which allowed us to deploy capital more quickly.

Our fund structure and operations were quite heavily influenced by the final point. There were three primary concerns that were being raised, namely:

1. How easy will it be to divest should things go wrong or if we have a change of strategy?

2. How will we incentivise the fund management team to ensure they put the organisation's interests ahead of their own?

3. How will we ensure that the fund's portfolio valuation is always fair and not over-inflated?

To address this, we set up the fund with a typical General Partner/ Limited Partner (GP/LP) structure, with all investments held in the special purpose vehicle we created as the GP and the Bank as the sole LP. As GP, the Bank then outsourced fund management responsibilities to SC Ventures. We also decided to appoint an independent third party as fund administrators and an independent valuation advisory firm.

THE QUEST FOR THE PIPELINE

We had our fund, we had our investment committee, and we had our defined processes. Now all we needed were companies to invest in. Our fund mandate was to invest in promising fintech opportunities in the Bank's ecosystem. Our sourcing process therefore needed to be heavily integrated with the Bank's businesses and functions, as well as with SC Ventures' eXellerator, which was the Bank's in-house startup accelerator initiative. There was no central repository of proofs of concept (POCs) the Bank was conducting, so we started calling businesses and functions to find out what was going on and whether they had leads for us. Today, we have started creating a pipeline, and have invested in a handful of companies to date.

While our investment committee and investment process are working, our pipeline-building process is still a work in progress. We spend a lot of time internally 'socialising' each investment recommendation before we take it to the investment committee. And while we are receiving more leads and proposals after becoming more well known, both internally and externally, we are now looking at tools to manage our pipeline. Sometimes we lose track of the conversation, which is not fair to the fintech firm that approached us.

We continue to learn. We continue to be a highly motivated workstream, and we continue to approach each investment as if it were our first. We have found that startups operate with a low-cost base and a lean operating model. Our controls and processes make it difficult to work with them, but we have found unique ways to overcome this while still being in line with Bank guidelines and regulations.

TAKEAWAYS

- While it is essential to invest in innovation, this also needs to have a financial return.
- Asking the right questions to create an operating model can help shape the team and keep everyone on track.
- There need to be clear steps for setting up an investment fund – ones that clearly communicate its goals.

11

CREATING OPTIONALITY FOR BANKING THROUGH NEW VENTURES

Alex Manson

CEO, SC Ventures

"... the clash of a platform business model against the conventional corporation model is a form of business model innovation."

SUSTAINING VERSUS DISRUPTIVE INNOVATION – PRODUCT INNOVATION VERSUS BUSINESS MODEL INNOVATION

Innovation is often confused with advancements in technology, or product innovation. It is also often called 'disruptive' when it is part of 'business as usual', a very important but less transformational form of innovation ('sustaining innovation'). 'Sustaining innovation' is not the same as 'disruptive innovation' and 'product innovation' is not the same as 'business model innovation'.

Sustaining or product innovation is not always visible, yet it is non-negotiable, with the penalty of irrelevance if not pursued.

It is what it takes to stay on top of the game: for example, digitising a Bank and serving customers the way they want to be served. This is where organisations should – and typically do – allocate most of their innovation resources. However, there is a low return on investment – financial institutions have spent billions digitising themselves, with little impact on their bottom line. That is because this type of innovation is easily replicable and does not differentiate any organisation from its competitors. It also means that any such innovation quickly comes to be expected of all businesses. This is hardly exciting from an investment perspective for the Chief Financial Officer (CFO) office, let alone shareholders. Yet it remains indispensable, as the consequence of not doing it would be to fall behind – an unacceptable outcome.

Disruptive innovation is different: it is harder to replicate and a lonelier journey, paved with mistakes and failures; but if successful, it has far more impact.

'Disruptive' tends to be an overused word in our industry and begs for a better definition. Experts have suggested that 'disruption' in business can happen in one of two ways:

1. A product providing a better way (VC – venture capital – firms say ten times better) than the current method of addressing customer needs emerges, disrupting its competitors. This has happened so often in history that, defined in this way, one might even say such product innovation actually falls under the umbrella of sustaining innovation.

2. The second type of disruptive innovation has little to do with the product itself, and more to do with the business model. As an incumbent, it can be hard to see business model innovation coming because the new product often does not appear particularly different. What is different is its way of operating, addressing the market, or earning revenues. For example, we would argue that the clash of the platform business model against the conventional corporation model is a form of business model innovation.

While the first type of disruptive innovation is, theoretically, do-able from within a corporation, this is not true of business model

Creating Optionality for Banking through New Ventures 69

innovation, no matter how willing the organisation is to embrace change and novel ideas. A major barrier is the organisational DNA: pursuing a business model different from the entrenched one is almost inevitably going to have to happen outside the corporation.

Returning to the genesis of SC Ventures (Chapter 1), we now better understand why the concept of 'banking the ecosystem' could not scale within the Bank fundamentally, due to the different business model. It simply had to be done outside the conventional organisation.

HOW IS THE CONVENTIONAL CORPORATION DIFFERENT FROM THE PLATFORM BUSINESS MODEL?

Leaving aside mission statements, and debate about which stakeholders to serve, a corporation's business model can be summarised as creating a product or a service (e.g., a mortgage product for a bank) and selling it at a profit to clients. It does this through sales channels, ranging from the conventional (bank branches) to the modern (the internet). We can think of this process as a pipe, where inputs (raw materials or information) are transformed into outputs (products or services) and sold to clients.

Understandably, a corporation wants to increase its revenues while simultaneously minimising costs, seeking to be ever more efficient. Entering a new market and tackling a new client base all serve to increase revenue. Automating processes and optimising channels serve to decrease costs. Importantly, in terms of its relationships with the outside world, the corporation is a closed universe, set out by the contracts that define it. Suppliers sell to it. It sells to clients. It is 'doing something to them' – but at its core, it is simply selling, through the pipe, to its customers.

Singularity University does a good job of outlining the difference between this conventional business model, known and refined since the industrialisation era, and the new platform business model: are you doing something *to* your customers (the most basic level), are you doing something *with* them (the next level), or are customers *doing it themselves*, as a community, on your platform? This third level is meant to achieve network effects and exponential growth, justifying the hopes and valuations of today's 'new economy' companies. (In the meantime, Steve Leonard, then CEO of Singularity, had joined our 'BrainTrust', alongside Claudia Zeisberger of INSEAD, Yen Yen Tan previously of Vodafone and David Gurle, founder and former CEO of Symphony.)

In a platform business model, the vertical pipe has disappeared and is replaced by many pipes, all connecting to the same platform. The platform does not necessarily sell to its users; rather, it administers an ecosystem of users and suppliers of services, enabling transactions in an open-architecture model where almost anyone can participate. Here the platform does little for participants; it is the participants, the community, that are doing the action for themselves. This may sound simplistic, but it is fundamental in understanding how the two models differ in organisational design, culture and DNA.

The *conventional corporation* is organised around vertical pipes. These pipes can be products or client segments (which is why many corporations call themselves 'client-centric'). The pipes are verticals, creating specialisation, which in turn creates efficiencies and economies of scale, minimises cost and maximises revenue. The corporation is also designed to protect itself and mitigate risk by regulating both the flow of information and the decision-making process.

This is what we often characterise as the 'chain of command', simplistically:

- People at the bottom of the organisational chart have little information.
- They pass on the little information they have to the level above them, and so forth, all the way to the top.
- The top layer then has all the information available in the organisation.
- This top layer can then make the few decisions required of them.
- Decisions then cascade back down to be put into action.

> *"The conventional corporation is organised around the vertical pipes."*

Meanwhile, the *platform business model* is designed around the community and to get it to scale, rather than trying to manage it. It administers the platform and lets the community manage itself, to a large extent. Therefore, companies that embrace this business model organise themselves differently:

- Information is made available to many people, as quickly as possible.
- This allows for decision-making by many, as quickly as possible.
- In fact, the decision-making has to be so fast that it is often devolved outside the organisation, to the community or is replaced by algorithmic decision-making on the back of the platform's data.
- Protecting the platform against the outside world is pointless if it prevents it from scaling and achieving network effects.

> *"The platform business model is designed to administer the community, and get it to scale, rather than trying to manage it."*

There may well be a point in the future when, as in the case of dot.coms, the bubble bursts and markets adjust, but some successful 'new economy' businesses do survive, forever changing how we live or do business. This would be the point when we look back and see our current period as the time when the platform business model challenged the corporations' business model.

A corporation serves the purpose of aligning several individuals, typically through the use of contractual arrangements (e.g., employment agreements, but also agreements with suppliers and distributors), around a shared purpose. This shared purpose is called a 'myth', or simply a 'story', by Yuval Noah Harari in his books *Sapiens* and *Homo Deus*, where he shows how the corporation can (fictionally) become a 'person' in itself.

Contrary to what some might advocate, I do not believe that the corporation business model is bad *per se* or is dying inexorably. It has certainly served a great purpose since the 19th century and may also serve a similar purpose in future, wherever the objective is to sell something to someone as efficiently as possible, concentrating resources and aligning individuals around this objective. It may also well be the right business model for apps or services plugging into platforms over time.

In fact, we could argue that it is easier to monetise apps or utilities, than it is to monetise platforms: notwithstanding their market valuations, they can be challenging profit and loss propositions – in some cases, such platforms could have developed an advertising business model that could become vulnerable for a variety of reasons, or they may use a data-driven monetisation model still subject to societal and regulatory validation.

This is not about attempting to predict the winner – will the platform model win, or is it just a fad, with old-fashioned business prevailing? Our answer is that we simply do not know. We can only make educated guesses based on history (think of the dot. com boom and bust), and the certainty of a non-linear evolution. This implies that platforms may not replace corporations as seamlessly as advocates, or private equity markets might predict. I am guessing that corporations and platforms will co-exist for some time, playing different roles in the business ecosystem. I would also predict that they will compete at times, but also co-operate, partner and merge sometimes. In fact, a conventional corporation could compete against, co-operate and partner with the same platform simultaneously, depending on the market, product or client segment.

There is, however, one existential implication for corporations from the 'platform challenge' we describe above: they must learn to play the game. First, corporations need to understand what they are up against. Second, they need to learn how to operate and survive in either form: either the corporation is reinvented as a platform; or the corporation is plugging into platforms (perhaps even, both at the same time).

This last point could be existential for some. My prediction is that some corporations may not survive the onslaught, because conventional organisations are not designed to cope with the platform model.

This is where the need for reinvention comes in. At SC Ventures, we called it 'rewiring the DNA in banking', but the challenge is

Creating Optionality for Banking through New Ventures 73

similar in every industry and almost every conventional corporation. It starts with the word 'DNA', from which we can derive organisational design and different ways of working, and the question is: what does it take for an existing and seemingly well-established corporation to 'rewire' its DNA?

> *"The question is: what does it take for an existing and seemingly well-established corporation to 'rewire' its DNA?"*

TOWARDS THE PLATFORM MODEL: OUR FIRST VENTURES REVOLVED AROUND BANKS AND PLATFORMS

As we reflected on disrupting and transforming financial institutions, we observed that the industry was not immune to a broader phenomenon in today's business world. This is the rise of platforms and their business model, which promised exponential growth on the back of their network effects.

We identify three primary scenarios for further thinking and experimentation. They are:

1. Platforms are a fad and banks are fine, provided they digitise and survive in a modified form that improves the customer experience. In this scenario, banks were still selling products to clients 'via the pipe', albeit a nicer and more efficient one.

2. Platforms win and end up owning the clients and controlling the client experience. Banks have no choice but to plug into the platforms, acting as a provider for some of the apps on that platform (banking as a service – BaaS)

3. The banks become platforms themselves, maintaining control of client ownership and experience, by administering an open ecosystem of solution providers.

It was clear that no one scenario could entirely describe the future, as they were all too simplistic. However, the general idea was that some version of these scenarios – perhaps as a function of the geography, client segment or product suite – could be a plausible evolution. Perhaps all three scenarios would end up playing out at the same time, in different situations, for different players. It was difficult to predict, but what we did know was that the market structure would evolve and that banks were going to have to learn to play on all these fronts.

The problem was that no corporate – including our bank – is equipped to adopt and experiment with these different models within their existing organisation. Clearly, such experimentation would have to take place outside of it. Rather than investing in startups and alternative models – typically with a limited learning effect and little transformational impact – our answer was to learn by doing. We decided to build *de novo* ventures positioned as startups outside the Bank, even though they would initially be backed by it. We thought of three ventures, each of which corresponded closely to a particular scenario.

Venture 1 was a digital bank, Mox, the ideation of which preceded SC Ventures. Mox was created after the Hong Kong Monetary Authority (HKMA) opened up its digital banking licensing regime and our local Retail Banking team decided to apply, even as the main local rival bank chose not to. This decision reflected the maturity of leadership, as it was clear that if Mox was to be successful, it had to address a different demographic segment than the Bank's existing retail business.

Venture 2 was project Nexus, a BaaS business where – enabled by a technology venture initially called Nexco (now audax) – we would plug our Bank, licence, and balance sheet into someone else's platform. Initially, there was a lot of resistance to the idea of targeting mass banking, something that was off strategy for the bank. It was also based in Indonesia, which is not one of the easiest markets to crack for a foreign bank. The regional CEO, stood behind our decision to go through with the idea of plugging our bank into some of Indonesia's large e-commerce platforms.

Venture 3 was Solv, an evolution of 'banking the ecosystem', which focused on India as its initial market and offered micro, small and medium-sized enterprises (MSMEs) a platform for 'conversational commerce' by simplifying their growth and operations across many business services, including but not limited to financing. This was a pure technology company and the very first time the

Bank had done anything like this: that is, build an open platform that was not led by financial services. Within two years, Solv had become one of the few projects driving the Bank's bold stand of uplifting participation of MSMEs.

This was a start – think of it as a model to structure initial thoughts on what ventures to build – but obviously did not begin to address the complexity of banking and financial services transformation. When complexity is daunting, go back to basics: in banking, it is about clients and perhaps more broadly societies' expectations from banks (see Chapter 1). We reflected on our North Star of 'Rewiring the DNA in banking' and came up with several themes representing plausible market evolutions and which we thought were relevant in the context of reinventing banking.

All of us had a high amount of conviction in these themes and they would help us decide what we were going to do – as well as what we were not here to do. Plus, the themes lent themselves to the creation of ecosystems: there could be more than one venture per theme, but the ventures within a theme were meant to reinforce each other and ideally plug into each other. This would accelerate each other's growth and impact.

We also linked our investments in third-party startups and partners of the Bank to the themes and thought of the combination of our ventures, and such portfolio companies as more powerful than any of them on their own (notwithstanding the need for every venture to be commercially viable in its own right).

At the time of writing this book, we had defined the following themes:

1. **Online Economy and Lifestyle**
   The rise and integration of the online economy is a key driver for growth. Financial services need to support digital lifestyles in such economies.

2. **SMEs and World Trade**
   World trade is a crucial engine for global welfare and Gross Domestic Product (GDP) growth, but small and medium-sized enterprises (SMEs) still struggle with inclusion in the global economy and access to the financial system.

3. Digital Assets
Digital assets are here to stay but in need of institutional adoption, requiring a robust and sustainable infrastructure.

4. Sustainability and Inclusion
Corporates and banks have yet to fully integrate sustainability and financial inclusion into their business models.

Since then, SC Ventures has incubated over 30 ventures. The initial and more advanced ones counted several hundred employees each and were building very meaningful businesses. At the other end, small teams were experimenting with prototypes to see if they could get further financial backing from us.

BUILDING VENTURES OUTSIDE THE ORGANISATION ... IS HARD AT THE BEST OF TIMES

Building ventures at arm's-length from the Bank was the very genesis of SC Ventures. Transforming banking was never going to happen within the Bank alone; some of it had to take place outside – or, rather, some hybrid of *inside* and *outside.*

When asked what is the one thing I wish I had known before starting this venture-building project, my semi-joking answer is usually: "I wish I had known it would be so hard!" It is not that knowing this would have changed anything, but I would have had a better idea of what to expect.

Venture building *is* hard. You are essentially in startup land, with those who build ventures being in the same position as the founders and entrepreneurs described in the previous chapters on fintech startups: strapped for cash and resources (in our case, by design), overburdened, immature, ill-equipped in so many ways, and, most importantly, dependent at all times on the next round of funding and what it takes to achieve it. We knew that the rate of survival of such enterprises is naturally low, and we accepted this risk.

The additional challenge in the context of corporate innovation was that Standard Chartered Bank backed our ventures. To be clear, this came with huge advantages: a calling card, an incubation

Creating Optionality for Banking through New Ventures 77

space, initial financial backing and, over time, the ability to scale the venture with help from the Bank (as the venture might also provide the Bank with adjacent opportunities). But as the ventures were subsidiaries of the Bank, we also needed to balance the requirements of the regulated banking group with the building of fintech startups.

The end-state of each venture was always meant to be an independent company, managed by a distinct management team and reporting to a board that would represent shareholder interests – including those of the Bank, and in most cases involving third-party shareholders as well. The attraction of third-party shareholders was help in scaling the venture financially and strategically, as well as in establishing corporate governance equivalent to that of a real company, as opposed to a project within the Bank. The path to an independent venture, however, involved incubation within the Bank and making a few tricky decisions.

Below describes the first and perhaps trickiest of such decisions – related to people – specifically in the context of independent ventures backed by a regulated financial institution.

DILEMMA NO.1: AN INSIDER OR OUTSIDER CEO AND TEAM MEMBERS?

It is tempting to assume that a corporation has plenty of professionals willing to jump into venture ideas. After all, ventures attract a lot of attention and are an ideal space for aspiring managers to prove and potentially rebrand themselves as innovative, entrepreneurial and action oriented. The corporation is also a tempting source of venture talent for another reason: staff will be familiar with (and it is hoped better able) to navigate its processes, as their network and political capital might provide them more leeway than an outsider.

Both assumptions are valid but are often outweighed by the fact that the CEO and the management team of a venture genuinely need an entrepreneurial spirit, and a completely different ability to take risks, operate amid uncertainty and be comfortable with the unknown associated with such ventures. It also needs people to give up their corporate careers – including sometimes titles, status and financial incentives – at least for some time. In other words, the crossover between entrepreneurs and existing corporate leaders is small.

As tempting as it was to appoint management teams from within the corporation, the right answer often turned out to be hiring people from outside the Bank and mixing insiders and outsiders in the management team. These outsiders were proven entrepreneurs, and while their startups may or may not have been hugely successful, they had typically learnt from the experience and could better deal with the process of running a venture. On the other hand, the insiders could help navigate the complexity of a regulated financial institution and better understand the context in which such regulations are imposed.

We were also mindful to prevent individuals from straddling roles across the Bank and SC Ventures. In its initial phase, a venture attracts attention and is an appealing opportunity for insiders to stand out. So, it is easy to attract part-time or temporary employees seconded to help with the launch or specific aspects of the venture. This can be a pragmatic solution, especially when compared to startups that do not have the luxury of a deep pool of experts on tap. But it is also a potential distraction, as people coming 'in and out' of the venture can create practical and cultural negatives. These people will not feel like they live or die by the venture, as they have the option to return to the corporation. Their level of commitment will not be the same as that of a proper founding team. For this reason, we were firm in insisting that as soon as a venture was formally backed and funded, with enough runway to justify a small team, people would be either in or out of the venture, but not straddling both. As always, a carefully balanced diversity was the best outcome. The ventures that failed to adopt this kind of diversity and mix of backgrounds ended up having to adjust.

DILEMMA NO.2: WHAT INCENTIVES SHOULD WE PROVIDE?

The next problem cropped up when individuals moved into the venture. On what terms should they come? Bankers – at least until recently – were used to earning higher salaries than startup founders, who instead owned equity in their enterprise. How much equity was necessary to justify transferring to the venture on a lower salary and fewer benefits? Should we 'grandfather' the first ventures with Standard Chartered Bank employees at the Bank's salary levels, then hire for newer ventures on different terms? And, if so, how should we justify different terms across similar enterprises?

We also wanted to avoid a cultural rift between former Bank employees and external hires by using different compensation models. It was always clear that the ventures' management teams would have to be incentivised with equity in their project, much like regular startup founders would. The question was: How much equity? Was it fair for someone to receive a 'bank-like' salary and equity at the same time? Would this create tensions in the team, or with the Bank itself? After long deliberations and taking some of our compensation experts in the Bank's HR unit on our journey, they agreed to submit a 'ventures remuneration framework' to the Bank board's remuneration committee. Eventually, they approved that SC Ventures could offer a combination of salary and equity, giving us the ability to optimise the two considering personal circumstances and the nature of the startup. We were betting that the ability to combine salary and equity in some fair and appropriate ratio would be a differentiating feature in competing for talent.

TAKEAWAYS

- There are three possible ways the industry can change in the future and as we do not know which one will prevail, a combination of scenarios will likely happen.

- The Bank has worked with ventures that adopt each of these scenarios and all have some successes.

- We ultimately succeeded in designing a framework to create business model optionality and new ways of working, while remaining within the Bank's regulation and risk perimeter.

12

VENTURE BUILDING: DESIGNING A CLEAR PATH FOR IDEAS

Harald Eltvedt

Operating Member

"The challenge was to make ourselves both agile and 'corporate'."

In every venture, we needed to embed ourselves at the right level of involvement, from the initial ideas phase onwards. This gave our entrepreneurial team space to experiment, learn and ultimately grow independently. We knew that enabling proper venture building would be quite distinctive from investing as a corporation. We needed an appropriate venture-building methodology that would take the context of a regulated bank into account, while not being impeded by the oversight. Entrepreneurs with success in mind like to go fast: they think fast, and they project fast. A venture is about an idea and the people who make it happen. But it is also about the people who adopt the idea or buy the product or service. So, it is always about people at the core. When it came to our entrepreneurs, they had to be the right people, with the right mindset and culture, and so we did our utmost to create processes that would serve them best.

As a regulated financial institution, we had to balance the speed you need with venture building, while not allowing for any short cuts in compliance and security. We had to shape the methodology routinely used in innovation labs, venture studios and successful startups in such a way, that it would also be fit for our environment, and sit within the Bank regulations, risk, governance, compliance, and cybersecurity frameworks. The challenge was to make ourselves both agile and 'corporate'.

We established strong convictions about the dos and don'ts in the methodology. We specifically did not want to build our projects in what some may consider to be the traditional 'corporate' way. The corporate way is often based on whatever – often thorough – research has been conducted, then getting a big budget and building the product in a waterfall way. To be entrepreneurial and consumer-centric, we needed to start small and lean, get feedback, iterate, and keep repeating until we knew the idea was worth pursuing. Only at this point would we scale and grow the venture.

Our approach was 'Lean Startup' together with human-centred design (HCD). HCD puts people in the centre of all processes, so we involved potential users from the design stage onwards. We would interview the people who would be the clients, to fully understand their needs, and the way they would eventually use the product, to inform our team about how to meet their needs.

While we kept to venture-building basics, we were also aware that the objective of our venture-building practice was to reinvent how banks serve society. The ventures had to fit our themes at that time: Online Economy and Lifestyle, small and medium-sized enterprises (SMEs) and World Trade, Digital Assets, Sustainability and Inclusion.

HOW COULD THAT BE DONE?

All strong ventures follow the same path: from the idea stage to incubation, acceleration, and commercialisation.

We applied the same methodology, staging our approach by using 'milestones', from idea to incubation, commercialisation and scaling. Ventures do start with great ideas, but it was important to

Venture Building: Designing a Clear Path for Ideas   83

resist the temptation to start scaling, before we meet the next milestone, and build a Minimum Viable Product (MVP), test it with users, iterate the MVP, and test it again. We needed to do this as often as it takes, to be certain that our MVP is worth transforming into a product at scale.

In 'phasing out' the process, we put our own 'BrainTrust' in each phase, as a way to get as much input from a diverse set of people and also clearance to the next stage. We wanted a group of people with experience and authority, no skin in the venture itself, but to help us validate every step by challenging, supporting – even at times coaching – the venture team towards the next stage. Importantly, the validation process would come from our team and from a different body, composed of Bank professionals as well as external advisors.

Our BrainTrust is a tribute to two high-level precedents. President Roosevelt's one, formed of Columbia Law School professors who played a key role in shaping the policies of the First New Deal (1933). And the one that Pixar movies started to 'Push towards excellence and root out mediocrity' in the earliest phases of a movie. The BrainTrust is not a committee. It will not take decisions. A core component of the BrainTrust are experts are from different fields and do not belong to the venture or the Bank. They bring their questioning and remarks freely, to provide the team with a different view. From the beginning, their contribution has been huge, both for improving the product and project, or informing and supporting our own decision-making.

BRAINTRUST BECAME AN INTEGRAL PART OF SC VENTURE'S CULTURE

As they progress, venture leads better understand the needs of their future buyers and the scope of the product. They are trained to test at each stage of the process and appreciate the special role of the BrainTrust. Leads also learn to appreciate the flow of questions, even tough ones, as a sign that the venture is at a stage where we are attempting to predict what could prevent its success in the market.

The phases include ideation to generate potential new business ideas; incubation to validate such ideas; acceleration to build the technology stack, set up the entity, and test it in the market; and commercialisation, once we were confident that we were 'on to something' so we can scale the ventures and their capabilities.

Ideation: This is about the 'North Star', the venture's one goal, which needs to be aligned with one or more of our high conviction themes. We also know that the best ideas are nothing without the right people, typically the ones who ask all the right and difficult questions about a specific issue. We must track weak signals, test them, and detect which ideas have the potential to grow into a successful venture, and which ones should be rejected outright. We involve stakeholders both from within the bank and external partners and bank clients, taking the original idea into the debate, using the Human Centred Design 'technique'. It is important to find out fast which ideas to reject so we do not waste precious time and resources on them. Once matured, the 'good' ideas can be presented to a small group of team members to make the decision to support them. At this point, the real work can start.

Incubation: A business that addresses tangible issues takes more than a good idea. Incubation takes about three months to turn the idea into an actual business proposition. Ventures are then 'tested' in terms of their business model, product benchmark and customer appetite etc, to validate assumptions made during the ideation phase: we typically 'prototype' the product and test it with people, asking specific questions and iterating based on their feedback. Only once a venture has a strong response to the original issue, does it get presented to a new panel or sometimes BrainTrust meeting, informing the decision to move it into the next phase.

Acceleration and commercialisation: This is a completely different chapter: first the venture is granted seed financing. This means we are no longer talking about an idea or a project, but rather a new business, with a real technology or product that is meant to solve a concrete issue in a successful way. A new entity is created at that stage and a proper team is formed, with its own set of objectives and key results (OKRs), with the main objective of gaining final validation to go to market. A new BrainTrust session happens

Venture Building: Designing a Clear Path for Ideas

at this stage, questioning whether the venture is at a point where commercialisation can start.

Each of these stages is important, yet none is enough to build a business unless the entire process has been mastered. Leadership rather than technology or architecture is critical for success. We had to push the venture team to its full potential, challenge it, and test their conviction – without muzzling it. And the BrainTrust helped us validate each of these stages.

While the Bank was invariably one of the initial backers, it was important that the whole process unfold outside of the Bank and its infrastructure – only this way, could we accommodate a lean startup methodology. This allowed us to bring flexibility and creativity while fulfilling the demands of a regulated financial institution, as we supported the venture in the background. This way, we believed we could be different from a traditional Corporate Venture builder, with a rigorous process that created better and faster decisions, while always communicating with the Bank for compliance purposes; but also, to acknowledge and absorb some of the changes we were initiating.

The BrainTrust is a way to have two circles complete one another: the inner circle oversees the venture, of its ongoing progress, while the outer circle of the BrainTrust comes at specific stages to look at the venture from a different angle. This process can change the dynamics of a venture.

BrainTrust is several things:

BrainTrust is NOT

- An echo chamber.

- A traditional investment committee.

- People criticising other people's work.

BrainTrust is

- About trust,

- trust between very engaged people,

- who can speak freely,

- and has its own dynamics.

- Adding value by highlighting issues and offering solutions to fix them.

- About belonging together in a free and chosen way.

The two circles work WITH one another to add value and discuss solutions.

The Venture circle has concrete work. Ideas come from various sources, we choose them and refine them until we are confident some might become a venture.

The BrainTrust circle is composed of people who are experts in their domain but are not part of the venture making. They see the whole idea at each stage and not how hard it has been to get to this point. They challenge the venture to keep it on its North Star mission while also pushing excellence in a non-authoritative way.

TAKEAWAYS

- Go to basics: start small and lean.
- Centre process on future acquires: test each phase, iterate, test again.
- Building ventures must have a standardised journey.
- Venture ideas are nothing without execution.
- Having external experts is key to broaden vision.

13

THE ROAD AHEAD: CORPORATE VENTURING *QUO VADIS?*

Prof. Claudia Zeisberger

Senior Affiliate Professor of Entrepreneurship & Family Enterprise, INSEAD

"Startups survive and thrive if they can navigate uncertainty, change course, pivot, adapt, and quickly react to new developments. Failure is not only normal but expected/anticipated — by investors — and understood as part of the game by founders."

SC Ventures has undoubtedly provided a fantastic learning opportunity for its parent organisation and senior management team since its launch in March 2018. An experiment at the start, it created a 'sandbox' or a laboratory which allowed this long-standing institution and its executives to experiment and watch some of their ideas turn into reality, receive some early funding and grow into real businesses, validated/ funded by external investors. Building a business from scratch, scaling it and seeing it go from captivity into the wild is a unique experience – certainly for a large institution. It requires an established financial institution to rethink its risk appetite and risk-taking capacity and asks for management to become comfortable with entrepreneurial risk taking – it is not a small task.

After all, the 'two-culture' issue is a reality: startups thrive on uncertainty, they pivot, change and react to new developments quickly, and failure is not only normal, but expected. Established corporations on the contrary do not appreciate failure and are rarely set up to be nimble and agile. Processes have been put in place to protect the incumbent, carefully watched by an army of compliance officers. Bringing in this up-start change agent is often hard to digest for a multinational parent company, especially a bank that operates in a tight regulatory environment. What to look forward to after those early steps by SC Ventures? What is realistic to expect in the coming years?

CONTEXT OF CORPORATE VENTURING

Let us look at some data. Historically, very few corporate venturing units have had the tenacity and survived any longer than SC Ventures to date. The few success stories usually cited – Intel capital deserving a shout-out here, investing in startups consistently since 1991 – should not drown out the high failure rate. As per INSEAD research from 2015, few corporate venturing teams have staying power beyond year five; a timeline too short to prove viability in building and growing startups, let alone showing an exit or financial returns.

Some teams spin out, leave the corporate home and establish themselves as independent investment vehicles with a variety of investors (LPs – limited partners or institutional investors). Most recently EON's and a few years ago, Airbus Ventures decided to go it alone; Next47 has been independent in its investment decision from its parent Siemens from the start. Others merged with R&D or the strategy department.

Looking at the number of venture investors in 2022, competition has certainly increased over the last five years. Not only was 2021 a record-breaking year in dollars deployed by corporate venture capital (CVC) globally (with an exceptionally high growth in Europe): in 2021, over 200 new corporate entities joined the venture capital party and more announced that they are interested in building a team which can help them execute. In line with the broader market, CVCs reduced their activity in 2023, but remained active – with some exploring the secondary market to add stakes in startups to their portfolio. Clearly CVC units live and die by the whims of the corporate which funds them/are responsible to the board of the corporate they serve, and more often than not, have a champion who ensures their survival.

Given this background, it is fair to the question the future and explore options ahead for the team.

What should be the goal of a corporate venture arm or any corporate venturing activity? Ultimately, it cannot be merely an undertaking focused on financial returns; returns of even the most successful venture or startup will barely make a dent in the share price of the parent company, even if a return in the hundreds per-cent of internal rate of return (IRR) were achieved. Over time, the 'mothership' needs to see advantages and receive viable inputs in its strategic decisions from the CVC team.

Therefore, the target has been for SC Ventures to weave itself tightly into the social and corporate fabric of Standard Chartered Bank and become part of the institution; this would mean that the Bank sees its activities as a vital part of its future business strategy and finds value in its innovation and value contribution.

Allow me to put this question to you, our readers, as I would do with my MBAs in class: What would be your advice? What would be a viable next step for SC Ventures?

To make this easier, let me provide additional information by giving you a glimpse behind the scenes of the daily work at SC Ventures:

SC VENTURES' STRUCTURE – THE HOW

SC Ventures's Investment Committee (IC) is to date formed of internal senior executives from Standard Chartered Bank. Nevertheless, prior to every IC meeting, every startup team has the opportunity to meet the 'BrainTrust', a committee made up of four external experts (all experienced early-stage investors with a financial industry background), 8 senior executives from Standard Chartered Bank and the members of the IC. Think of the BrainTrust as an advisory board on steroids, where the startups are not only exposed to critical questions, but also receive advice, guidance and valuable feedback. Once the startup team members leave the room, the BrainTrust members deliberate and share their vision for the business idea, and their concerns about the riskiness of the venture. IC members can listen to the frank and honest input from independent advisors without skin in the game.

One question for future changes comes to mind: should the BrainTrust merge with the IC – or is there value to have access to external experts in the startup space – but then make the actual investment decisions by a purely internal team?

SC Ventures' model to date has been to leverage the ideas emerging from its parent company's employees i.e., a captive pool for idea generation.

Venture building as done by SC Ventures right now can of course be enhanced with the help of external parties – advisors who kickstart the process of ideation, team building and execution. How external parties are being received by the internal team; how much learning there is over the long run are questions often asked by corporations. SC Ventures continues to experiment with Venture Building and has had good experiences to date. But can the existing model truly transform an organisation? Is it time to expand the activities and consider a platform model? Let me explain this idea:

As an international player, Standard Chartered Bank may well invite other financial institutions to join their sandbox and explore how to improve the way financial markets and services can be improved. Bringing bright minds around the table might create an energetic and interesting ecosystem with benefits for all parties involved. But one wonders if the innovation created in such an environment would be relevant for Standard Chartered Bank – or would the output suffer from the issue of 'too many cooks in the kitchen'?

It is time for the SC Ventures team to consider the success stories in its portfolio, decide on suitable exits and then take the lessons learned from the early years and grow its activities to the benefit of the parent company?

TAKEAWAYS

- Corporate Venturing requires an established financial institution to rethink its risk appetite and risk-taking capacity.

- Historically, very few corporate venturing units have had the tenacity to survive for longer than five years.

- The SC Ventures model has used both an Investment Committee (IC) to deliberate investment decisions, and a BrainTrust of external experts, to give impartial advice and feedback.

14

SOLV: A B2B E-COMMERCE MARKETPLACE FOR SMALL BUSINESSES

Gautam Jain[a] and Amit Bansal[b]

[a]Operating Member
[b]CEO, SOLV India

Solv is a business-to-business (B2B) digital commerce platform addressing the growth challenges of micro, small and medium-sized enterprises (MSMEs) by connecting buyers and sellers and providing access to financing and business services.

> *"[We] chose a unique brand name for ourselves that would speak volumes about what the team dreamt of accomplishing."*

SOLV's vision: To accelerate India's economy by solving growth challenges for every small or medium-sized enterprise in India.

SOLV's mission: SOLV aims to accelerate growth for India's 63 million+ MSMEs[1] by leveraging technology and data to empower businesses to create more jobs, trade, and contribute to India's growing economy.

SOLV is an India-based B2B e-commerce marketplace for MSMEs. The SOLV platform facilitates commerce in a trusted environment while easing access to finance and business services through one seamless digital experience. MSMEs on the SOLV platform can discover, connect and do business with other verified MSMEs and take advantage of on-demand working capital also.

THE SOLV JOURNEY

SOLV was formally incorporated in January 2019. However, the ideation process started much earlier with a small core team operating out of a meeting room in the Standard Chartered Global Business Services (GBS) office in Bangalore, India. As of September 2024, the SOLV platform employs over ~400 people, has over ~400,000 customers and records thousands of orders daily.

Since its inception, SOLV has been focused on India's MSME ecosystem. The reasons for this are as follows:

1. **The opportunity:** India is home to over 63 million MSMEs, which are powering the country's economic growth. They contribute ~30 per cent of the nation's Gross Domestic Product (GDP), account for 45 per cent of exports and employ over 110 million people. However, this segment faces a huge credit gap of US$355 billion[2].

2. **The challenge:** India's MSME sector faces a host of problems that stifle growth. As a result, over 95 percent of businesses in India are micro-enterprises – resulting in a phenomenon called the 'missing middle', which represents a dearth in the number of MSMEs. This sector is also largely untouched by technology.

3. **Favourable shifts at the macro level:** The introduction of initiatives such as demonetisation, the Goods and Services Tax (GST) and Aadhaar (the world's largest biometric system, implemented in India, which is a 12 digit unique identity number that is obtained voluntarily from residents of India), coupled with the rise of smartphones and cheap data, have made the Indian MSME ecosystem incredibly data-rich within a very short time.

SOLV was able to identify the opportunity and set out its vision to help India's small businesses accelerate growth by leveraging the power of technology and data.

As SOLV became an independent venture, we started to dig deeper and discovered that MSMEs in India have a daily grapple with several fundamental challenges. Notably, access to credit was challenging but we discovered several other issues, which we will cover in a moment. We gathered feedback by talking to small business owners and visiting industry events. Then we decided to increase the scale and scope of our market research efforts in the first half of 2019 by engaging one of India's leading market research agencies, Dun & Bradstreet, to conduct an in-depth study. A total of 500 MSMEs across 16 cities, nine industries and five sectors participated in the study, the findings of which helped set the foundations of our business and hone our positioning.

We realised that the challenges faced by MSMEs can be broadly categorised into three buckets:

1. **Access to new customers:** Most small businesses have a small customer base limited to where they are based. Their ability to expand their business is constrained by the lack of ways they can gather customer leads.

2. **Access to finance:** There is a lack of formal financial documentation but lengthy processes and a high collateral requirement. This means Indian MSMEs are left out of the formal credit fold and are unable to get credit when they need it most.

3. **Time-consuming, manual business operations:** Most small businesses in India are owner-managed, which means that it is the business owner who spends a lot of time running the day-to-day operations, leaving them little time to grow the business. These business owners also lack access to professional services and software solutions as these are typically expensive and not tailored for small businesses.

At SOLV we decided to attack all three challenges by creating a unique B2B e-commerce marketplace that would assist MSMEs in the following ways:

- Helping them to connect and do business with each other. A manufacturer/factory owner can showcase its products and reach customers across the country through this marketplace. A retailer can reach scores of new suppliers and access a wide selection of products at the best price.

- Helping MSMEs to get access to credit by connecting them with the right financial services partner. This makes the process quick and easy. It also means they have the cash to order the supplies they need to meet new orders and grow.

- Serving tier 2 and 3 retailers through anchor-led supply chain finance.

The SOLV B2B marketplace was built on five key foundational principles:

1. **Customer focus:** All features of the platform have been designed, and evolved, with the customer in mind.

2. **True marketplace:** SOLV's vision has always been to digitise India's B2B supply chains and make them more efficient. Therefore, our platform was designed to connect buyers and sellers in a trusted online environment. Similarly, on the financing side, the platform was designed to be financial institution compatible and to give the MSME single-window access to multiple providers.

3. **Easy-to-use interface:** We first envisaged the SOLV platform as a mobile app with a chat interface, as small business owners are usually on their phones and are most comfortable with chat-based messaging systems.

4. **Tech-enabled:** The SOLV platform was built using artificial intelligence/machine learning (AI/ML) technologies so that the data generated by the scores of MSMEs using the platform in the future can serve them more effectively. We also recognised the need to build a robust end-to-end fulfilment infrastructure that will support growth in terms of operations and logistics.

FROM BETA TO GO-LIVE

The SOLV app was initially launched in beta mode on the Google Play Store and >8,000 small and medium-sized enterprises (SMEs) joined between February to August 2020 (mostly in the staples and fast-moving consumer goods [FMCG] category). We got approval to go live in September 2020 and have seen tremendous growth since then.

We closed 2020 with 20,000 onboarded customers and over US$5 million in gross transaction value (GTV). We added new categories, namely: apparel, home furnishing, footwear, consumer electronics, and very recently added toys and sports. The invoice-based financing solution and Embedded Finance was launched in January 2020 to help the thousands of MSMEs using the platform to get access to short-term credit. Three leading new-age lenders – Indifi, ePayLater and Davinta – partnered with SOLV to extend credit to SOLV buyers via Embedded Finance.

SUPPLY CHAIN FINANCE

In line with its vision of helping SMEs to accelerate growth, SOLV has developed a supply chain finance (SCF) platform. The idea behind this platform is to help smaller dealers and distributors get timely, collateral-free financing at attractive interest rates by leveraging their anchor relationships. This helps dealers with improved liquidity and greater stock-holding capability, which is particularly useful during peak buying seasons. The platform ensures end-to-end transparency, transaction visibility, secure and immutable transactions, and tokenisation of invoices.

SOLV AND COVID

B2B Marketplace: India's lockdown to stem the spread of COVID affected many business owners, and disruption in the supply chain caused massive shortages. *Kiranas* (local grocery shops) and medium to large retailers had to close their businesses.

India's government allowed stores supplying essentials to remain open. However, retailers and grocers did not have the channels and connectivity to buy their supplies from those higher up in the chain – namely, manufacturers, traders and wholesalers.

SOLV helped sellers who were already on their platform to deliver basic, daily essentials such as groceries, fresh produce and FMCG products to both existing and new buyers. For suppliers who could not do business with their regular buyers, SOLV helped them to connect with new buyers. The objective of the lockdown was to enforce public health safety; therefore, even if retailers were open, going out and getting supplies posed a serious health risk. The SOLV team further helped retailers supply large residential communities, non-profit organisations and hospitals. SOLV was actively engaged in assisting small businesses to operate, and supported people to access much-needed supplies.

Financial Services: SOLV announced the launch of its COVID Emergency Credit Line Programme in association with FICCI-CSME (India's leading national industry body) for MSMEs that are helping the nation to fight the COVID pandemic. The nationwide lockdown badly impacted the business sustainability of MSMEs due to a lack of cash flow to meet their fixed costs. In this scenario, the COVID Emergency Credit Line was aimed at easing the sector's financial pain.

Partnership: SOLV partnered with Bangalore-based Akshay Patra Foundation, one of India's largest non-governmental organisations (NGOs), to connect Akshay Patra to its robust network of MSMEs who were supplying essential goods. The partnership helped maintain the smooth delivery of supplies to the foundation's kitchens. It also sustained several *Kirana* stores and small businesses engaged in the manufacturing and distribution of essential food supplies. With the partnership, SOLV helped Akshay Patra during the COVID lockdown with sourcing materials for its COVID Relief Feeding Programme, which aims to support the needy with one 10 million cooked meals and 500,000 packaged grocery kits.

This initial success and experience led to the forging of a long-term partnership for SOLV to support Akshay Patra with its supply-chain services and sourcing partners.

SETTING UP A BRAND FROM SCRATCH

While SOLV's registered entity name is Standard Chartered Research and Technology India Pvt Ltd, we took an unconventional approach and chose a unique brand name for SOLV that would speak volumes about the team's goals. The name suggests solving challenges, and the rationale behind designing the logo was to instil optimism, openness and accessibility to growth for the MSME segment. The open 'O' is a symbolic representation of freedom from the challenges, leading MSMEs to focus on the growth of their business. It also represents the opening of possibilities for our clients to grow without limits.

THE ROAD AHEAD AND AMBITION

India is at the cusp of a major digital revolution; half the population has smartphones and data connectivity. The government has put in place progressive policies for the growth of digital and startup ecosystems. While the last decade was marked by the rise in business-to-consumer (B2C) e-commerce players, the next decade will be all about bringing the power of e-commerce to the B2B space.

SOLV is poised to hit 600,000 MSMEs on its platform by 2025. It has forged strong domestic partnerships with several regional and national seller brands across categories, logistics providers, banks and non-banking financial companies (NBFCs). We are using a multi-pronged approach to attract new customers and drive platform stickiness through loyalty programmes. We are expanding our scale of operations by adding new cities and categories. Plus, we are adopting new business models such as direct-to-retail (DTR) and advertising that will help to grow revenues.

SOLV is also geared for international business by leveraging Standard Chartered's global presence.

> **TAKEAWAYS**
>
> - SOLV has provided a solution to enable growth in India's micro, small and medium-sized enterprise (MSME) market by opening up new avenues for business, credit, and partnerships.
> - SOLV played a crucial role in making sure small businesses could survive the pandemic lockdown and deliver essential supplies to communities.
> - Market research is crucial to spot the non-obvious problems and opportunities that a new approach can help fix.

NOTES

1. https://www.ifc.org/en/stories/2024/small-business-big-impact

2. https://www.ifc.org/en/stories/2024/small-business-big-impact

15

AUDAX: TRANSFORMING BANKING TECHNOLOGY FROM LEGACY TO LIMITLESS

Kelvin Tan

CEO, audax Financial Technology

audax is a cloud-native digital 'bank in a box', boasting an end-to-end digital banking platform with modularised capabilities that complements existing banking systems, deployed as a scalable layer within bank or scale-as-a-service.

> *"Above anything else, you need a tremendous amount of resilience. You will be told 'No' or that 'it cannot be done' at multiple intervals. You need to be able to get up and get around obstacles and keep the endgame in mind."*

FROM HUMBLE BEGINNINGS

The story of audax begins not as a company, but as an idea. During my time at Standard Chartered Bank, it became clear that two complementary macro pressures would affect all banks, almost without exception.

The two macro pressures are:

- to significantly increase return on equity (ROE) on their retail and small and medium-sized enterprise (SME) balance sheets through scale and lowering costs to acquire and serve.

- to significantly upgrade their incumbent technology solution to deliver the former. A complete digital transformation and business model overhaul was needed for all banks to penetrate all emerging markets, where digitally savvy populations are rapidly entering the financial mainstream via notions of Digital Banking or banking as a service (BaaS) that enables Embedded Finance. This realisation sparked the inception of audax, a digital banking platform that helps incumbent banks and financial institutions (FIs) scale and modernise at speed with minimal risk to their existing technology estate.

AUDAX – SUPERCHARGING THE FUTURE OF FINANCE

audax means bold and courageous in Latin, which underpins the fundamental characteristics we value in the company. We built a team with a bold mission: to empower banks and FIs to thrive in the digital age.

In the next paragraphs, we will trace:

1. audax's journey from its origins to its current standing.

2. Industry challenges audax aims to solve.

3. Industry breakthroughs we have had.

4. Why incumbent banks and FIs should work with us.

Vision	Supercharging banks and FIs with modern digital financial services to enhance their financial capabilities and unlock opportunities for growth
Mission	Empowering banks and FIs to scale and modernise at speed so they can focus on their core business

THE JOURNEY OF AUDAX

The story of audax is a testament to the power of innovation, and the incredible support of forward-thinking partners and sponsors. With the support of Standard Chartered Group CEO, Bill Winters, SC Ventures played a pivotal role in transforming this idea that I had back in 2018, into the audax that we know today.

Not many would know, but the genesis of audax started with Standard Chartered nexus (SC nexus), a white-label BaaS proposition that is currently live in Indonesia. As an 'intrapreneur' of the Bank, I built both SC nexus and audax from scratch, where SC nexus was the new business model that enables the Bank to create new revenue streams from their BaaS proposition, with audax as the technology capability that powered SC nexus.

audax's full-stack technology platform propelled Standard Chartered (through SC nexus) as the first global bank to offer BaaS in Asia, a pioneering feat that laid the foundation for the spin-off of audax. We have won multiple awards over the past six years, and this serves as a testament to the quality and standards that we have as a team.

This desire to continuously be bold and courageous is also what sets audax apart. We possess a deep understanding of the technology, security, resilience and compliance requirements of a modern digital banking platform, having built our solution from the ground up within a major global FI. The user-friendly, plug-and-play solution, enabling rapid modernisation and scalability for incumbent banks, was also another key proposition of audax, because we understand the pain points and pressures that incumbent banks face.

THE CHALLENGES WE SOLVE

The winds of change are sweeping through the financial industry, where banks and FIs are racing to achieve high ROE and scalable digital models, making modern digital transformation a non-negotiable. Banks today face competition not just from traditional rivals, but also from nimble challenger banks, technology companies and a wave of fintech startups offering capabilities from e-wallets to digital payments. The game has changed – using traditional banking strategies no longer suffice amid declining global banking ROE.

To compete effectively, incumbent banks and FIs need to solve two critical challenges / macro pressures mentioned earlier:

1. **Building a scalable digital business model:** Banks need to pivot and build digital business models, deliver superior returns, while supporting future growth through scalability and low costs of acquisition and servicing. Achieving scale is crucial, not just for customer experience and efficiency, but also for building a robust data infrastructure that fuels continuous adaptation.

2. **Modernising legacy infrastructure:** Incumbent banks must also recognise the importance of strategic technology investments. Upgrading aging systems is a costly and complex undertaking, and patchwork solutions are often ineffective and create further complications down the line. Banks could either consider a) an overhaul of their technology systems by building the entire technology platform in-house, which is expensive and takes years to complete; b) purchase capabilities from multiple vendors, incurring high costs and bearing the risk of integration and multi-dependences; or c) consider modern solutions such as audax's proven solution with live use cases, boasting a fully integrated and scalable software that is much cheaper and faster to deploy.

THE ACHIEVEMENTS WE HAVE MADE

In a significant milestone, audax enabled Bukalapak, Indonesia's leading e-commerce platform, to venture into digital banking services (named BukaTabungan) through an ecosystem partnership with Standard Chartered Bank. This collaboration led to *a threefold expansion of Standard Chartered Bank's customer base in Indonesia within six months*, presenting a substantial growth opportunity arising from this partnership.

BukaTabungan's digital banking service combines the extensive reach of Bukalapak's platform with the cutting-edge technology of Standard Chartered Bank's BaaS solution. This partnership has provided inclusive, easy, and secure digital banking services to Bukalapak's ecosystem of over 110 million users and 20 million business owners. With BukaTabungan's Current Account and Savings Account (CASA) services, it became one of the first digital banking services to offer an end-to-end, fully digital Know Your Customer (KYC) onboarding process. In 2023, BukaTabungan expanded its offerings to include debit cards, as well as lending capabilities that are currently available to specific whitelisted users.

Through BaaS and BukaTabungan, Standard Chartered Indonesia was able to:

1. Attract 98 percent new-to-bank customers, expanding into new customer segments.

2. Attain 85 percent application approval rate; of which 97 percent of account openings are done in real time.

3. Implement onboarding processes in as fast as 2 minutes, significantly reducing onboarding costs.

THE AUDAX ADVANTAGE

audax was built to eliminate the uncertainty from bank modernisation with a plug-and-play infrastructure that keeps technical debt low and avoids the need for expensive system overhauls. audax also enables dual-mode evolution for banks and FIs, allowing them to simultaneously modernise their legacy infrastructure while rapidly deploying new digital services. This dual approach ensures continuity and stability, while also fostering innovation and agility. As we were spun out from SC Ventures, our technology is inherently compliant by design, aligned to security, resilience and compliance standards both globally and locally, ensuring regulatory peace of mind.

KEY VALUE PROPOSITIONS

audax is not just a solution provider but a partner in banks and FIs' digital transformation journey, offering the expertise and technology needed to thrive in the ever-evolving financial landscape.

Looking back, audax has come a long way since its roots in 2018. The desire to push frontiers now propels audax as we lead and pave the way forward for future innovations and expansions in the financial industry.

The Only Live Full-Stack Digital Banking Platform	Unlike competitors with limited features, audax offers a comprehensive platform that can solve for all three key use cases: digital banking, BaaS, and legacy infrastructure modernisation.
Rapid Go-to-Market	Our full-stack solution allows clients to launch within 6-9 months, eliminating the need to integrate various point solutions.
Global Security & Compliance	With a proven track record of success for Standard Chartered Bank in multiple markets, audax targets cutting-edge security and compliance on a global and local scale.
Banking Expertise	Spun out from SC Ventures, our team has a deep understanding of the complexities of banking, allowing us to tailor solutions that address the unique challenges and demands of traditional FIs.
Functional BaaS Business Model	Led by individuals with a successful track record at deploying a live BaaS solution for Standard Chartered Bank, audax offers unparalleled experience in implementing BaaS business models. We are your guide to unlocking exponential growth in the digital age through Embedded Finance.

TAKEAWAYS

- audax is a cloud-native digital 'bank in a box', that complements existing banking systems, and aims to empower banks and FIs to thrive in the digital age.

- audax enabled Bukalapak, Indonesia's leading e-commerce platform, to venture into digital banking services (named BukaTabungan) through an ecosystem partnership with Standard Chartered Bank.

- Banking as a service (BaaS) business models can be implemented, that can unlock growth in the digital age through Embedded Finance.
- The plug-and-play infrastructure of audax avoids the need for expensive system overhauls and ensures regulatory peace of mind due to its inherent 'compliance by design'.

16

REWIRING THE DNA THROUGH EXPERIMENTATION

Gurdeep Singh Kohli

Operating Member

"Dreaming big was very important for us in the spirit of 'bringing the Bank along'."

Back in November 2017, when Alex Manson was still the Global Head of Transaction Banking, we were in his office every evening designing the blueprint for SC Ventures. After a fair amount of deliberation, we concluded that venture building needed to be an integral, non-negotiable, part of SC Ventures. The conviction stemmed from an earlier project, 'Banking the Ecosystem'. While the idea had been good, it did not take off as we had planned. This was partly because it was treated like an internal project and a product, rather than as a completely new business model.

We needed venture building to experiment with business models 'outside' the Bank in order to rewire the DNA in banking.

These business models were related, but not restricted, to financial services. After all, banking could no longer afford to operate as a closed industry without connecting with different ecosystems. Organisations that have successfully transformed themselves have done so by continuously creating new businesses that are unrelated even to the core. It was not about building new products as part of business as usual, or about creating efficiencies in the way we did banking. It was about setting up independent ventures or startups that are commercially viable and investible propositions.

> *"It wasn't about building new products as part of business as usual, or about creating efficiencies in the way we did banking. It was about setting up independent ventures or startups that are commercially viable and investible propositions."*

There were two main goals. The first was to create a portfolio that would contribute meaningfully to the valuation of the Bank and could change the shape of the Bank's future revenues. The second goal was to drive a mindset and culture change within the Bank. While it is too early to declare success against the first objective, we did succeed in changing the mindset and culture.

I was in Group Strategy before joining SC Ventures. Most traditional global banks focus on the affluent and high net worth segment, whereas the mass-market segment is where large local banks have the dominant share given their exhaustive branch presence. audax completely changed this when it showed a different way to do this, by using partnerships and technology. We were one of the first global banks to announce our intentions in the digital assets space when we set up Zodia Custody, the institutional-grade custodian for digital assets. Through SOLV, we approached the micro, small and medium-sized enterprise (MSME) problem in a completely different way by setting up a technology company to provide an open platform for commerce and financing.

It was only a matter of time before other parts of the organisation, across markets, started to respond with their own initiatives and engaged with SC Ventures for client co-creation ideas. This is exactly what Bill Winters wanted. We were a catalyst for the organisation – both in terms of what and how to approach business models.

DEFINING BUSINESS MODELS

We did not start by boxing ourselves into what we will and will not do – that would have been inconsistent with the spirit

Rewiring the DNA through Experimentation 111

of experimentation. We started with only a couple of ideas and the rest emerged over time. Within two years, we incubated over 30 ideas across our high-conviction themes, client bases and markets, with now a number of commercially launched ventures in full operation.

These high-conviction themes drove some of the business models we backed:

- Client lifestyle and client experience will be at the centre of digital business models, and the lines between traditional client segments will blur. This was our core belief when we designed Mox (digital bank) and Autumn (digital retirement platform).

- MSMEs will be the biggest driver of welfare and equality. The segment's challenges can be better solved through open platforms built around partnerships. This led to the setting up of SOLV and our announcing a supply chain financing partnership.

- Digital assets are here to stay, giving rise to more uses and institutional adoption. This, in turn, will lift institutional standards. Zodia Custody and Libeara reflected this belief.

- As online commerce becomes an inseparable part of everyone's life, customers will expect more from their e-commerce channels. E-commerce players themselves will need a range of financial and payment services. Standard Chartered nexus, our banking as a service (BaaS) venture, and Zai, our payments venture, were built around the e-commerce ecosystem.

- Banks will search for their Amazon Web Services equivalent to scale and monetise their existing capabilities. One venture, letsbloom, targeted fintechs to provide them with a 'bank-grade and bank-ready' infrastructure.

- As global organisations committed to sustainability and inclusion, they will need to rethink how to build and invest in viable business models. Banks have a huge role to play and will need to work with like-minded clients.

The above themes and beliefs covered the full range of client segments, from individuals to corporates to institutions.

WHY BUILD FROM WITHIN THE BANK, WHEN IT IS SO DIFFICULT?

We often get asked these questions: Does it make sense for a bank to build new business models? Can a bank even compete in this space? Does it have any edge over fintechs, which are faster and nimbler and do not carry the regulatory requirements? As Alex mentioned, corporate innovation, especially within a bank, is challenging; however, we have some significant advantages. Let me elaborate.

Building ventures for and within a bank is indeed hard. After all, banking is one of the most heavily regulated industries. Banks are the trusted custodians of assets and data; they move money across borders and play a huge role in countries' economies. International banks need to manage the expectations of multiple regulators across their business – in 59 markets for Standard Chartered Bank, to be precise. They need to adopt global risk management practices, such as the three lines of defence, or domicile-specific regulations such as the Senior Managers Regime, which stresses individual accountability. Over and above these requirements, a bank with over 150 years of existence (or any corporation with a long history) has built processes and standards that are deeply embedded into its DNA.

This all impacts the speed, direction and cost of innovation. It would be pointless to compare corporate venture building with building startups in a 'garage'. Venture building in a non-banking corporation is easier than in a bank. Simply look at how many new business models have come out of banking compared to other sectors. I was often told by venture leads, especially during the early stages, that if they were to do it again, they might reconsider the decision to build within the bank. However, they may not have realised that its advantages could outweigh the early pain and costs over time.

The following are some of the advantages:

- **The bank provides the seed capital.** Entrepreneurs who have had to raise money will appreciate the sort of temporary 'safety net' a bank's support provides to experiment with an idea.

- **There is easier access to certain clients.** External entrepreneurs could only dream of the ease with which a venture backed by a

Rewiring the DNA through Experimentation

bank could get an audience with decision-makers with potential corporate clients.

- **A venture backed by a bank carries more weight and credibility.** Although some investors – venture capitalists, in particular – tend to dislike a corporation owning a venture.

- **For some ventures, the bank could provide a pool of clients to test a proposition.** A venture only relying on bank clients would not be viable; but having access to select clients for testing a proposition, or even access to early adopters, may help the venture take off. The bank itself may even be a potential client.

- **Do not underestimate the power of the brand.** Some ventures have capitalised on a bank's brand strength by stating their relationship explicitly – for example, Mox, the digital bank in Hong Kong, declares "by Standard Chartered".

- **Easier access to global talent, including a network of advisors.** We appointed some high-profile independent directors to the board of some of our early-stage ventures. That would not have been possible for a startup still trying to make its mark.

- **The aspects that make it harder for a venture to take off initially can become strengths over time.** Key factors that differentiate bank-backed ventures from 'garage' fintechs include having access to high-grade security, infrastructure and risk management. Clients often attach a premium to a bank-backed venture with such high initial standards, in time offsetting the initial expense and challenge of building it.

In summary, the long-term advantages of building a venture from within a bank should outweigh potential inefficiencies. We are seeing some early confirmations of this bet or conviction, such as with Mox and Zodia.

FROM DOUBTS TO UNICORN DREAMS

The Bank's expectations of SC Ventures changed very quickly. When we started, SC Ventures was seen as just another lab where people wore T-shirts to work and were doing 'cool stuff'. One of my ex-colleagues, who congratulated me on making the 'big' move, then lamented that while I was 'having fun', he was struggling to drive revenues which were the real deal. People often commented on our dress code and would ask where my tie was. (I had always previously colour co-ordinated my tie with my turban.)

In the industry, the chance of a startup becoming a success – a 'unicorn' – is less than 1 percent, and it takes several years to achieve this. The implication for us was clear: even if we had a marginally higher success rate, we needed to incubate a large number of ventures. But we did not expect the Bank to be patient with us and give us so much time.

Soon, people started to see that we meant business and that while we were a fun team, we were serious about rewiring the DNA in banking. Within six months of launching SC Ventures, the same colleague who had described what I was doing as 'having fun' asked to join SC Ventures and wanted to know when we would be announcing our first unicorn. (This is sometimes, and unfortunately, the only benchmark people have for credible innovation effort.)

TOP OF THE FUNNEL: THE CHALLENGE OF SOURCING

We started with two to three venture ideas that came from the founding members of SC Ventures. As we grew, we experimented with different sources, with varying degrees of success – meaning that no one sourcing approach was more successful than any other.

We learnt that we had to spend disproportionately more time on sourcing and evaluating the people, than on the idea. This might seem like conventional wisdom, but we needed to go through the journey. In doing so, we ignited the entrepreneurial spirit. People across the Bank reached out to us with their business model pitches. Some pivoted from our Intrapreneurs Programme by first solving a bank problem that then eventually became a venture. The response to 'venture challenges' was outstanding. It was great to see enthusiastic teams, across all levels in the organisation, pitching propositions to panels comprising very senior stakeholders.

These stakeholders were learning, as this was all new for them. But they encouraged employees to participate and to dream big, which was important for us in the spirit of 'bringing the Bank along'.

When the intrapreneurs were committed, the internal sourcing worked very well. When the CardsPal venture lead, Siam Yeong Harng, was given a small sum of pre-seed funding as an encouragement to keep going with his idea, he quit his job and convinced us to hire him in SC Ventures. There was no looking back. Of course, we could not do that with every intrapreneur who had an idea. Not having dedicated resources did impact the speed and quality of progress, but I would say it was the lead's hunger and commercial sense of a venture that impacted the progress.

Even when we fully backed an idea to production, we found the intrapreneurs hesitating to let go of their job or title within the Bank. This straddling between Ventures and the 'day job' was a recipe for disaster. The safety net a corporation provides might help get started, but it becomes a blocker if people hold on to it. So, we started looking outside for ideas and, more importantly, for teams. This was either through client co-creation, or an inorganic approach and buying a company to recruit its employees. The belief was that this could solve the problem of both talent and speed to get ventures off the ground.

DECISION-MAKING BODIES

As we started making noise, questions were being asked about governance – after all, we were part of a global bank operating in a regulated industry across multiple territories. We were also a bit surprised by how fast the ventures portfolio grew. The biggest mistake would have been to default to the Bank's ways of working – not because something was wrong with it, but that it did not fit our purposes for ventures. Governance is non-negotiable; but more often than not, good governance is confused with more governance. We had to learn as we built – and learn quickly.

> *"Governance is non-negotiable; but more often than not, good governance is confused with more governance."*

Yet, the questions kept coming: Who makes the decisions to fund a venture? What are the stages of ventures? How are we managing risk? How are we tracking the portfolio? What partnership conversations are we having? How are we managing reputational risk? What policies and standards need to be applied? Are we saying 'No' enough? What should be the subsidiary governance?

Large organisations draw comfort from having committees make decisions, while simultaneously wishing for simpler decision-making. In the beginning, when someone proposed a committee for each major decision – one for funding, one for risk, and one for monitoring – thankfully, Bill pushed back. We started with two main 'central' bodies: a BrainTrust as a forum for evaluating proposed business models; and a committee for risk and policies approvals (SCV Risk Committee – SCVRC). Once the venture becomes commercially operational and mature, the accountability belongs to the venture management team and the venture board.

The concept of a BrainTrust was inspired by the book *Creativity, Inc.: Overcoming the Unseen Forces That Stand in the Way of True Inspiration*, by Amy Wallace and Edwin Catmull, which Alex made us read. We loved the idea of having a BrainTrust so much, that we shamelessly adopted it as one of our governance bodies. BrainTrust was intended to be an advisory body that would provide a venture with candid feedback and identify all the ways it could fail. It was not about creating solutions – that was left to the venture teams. Over time, we added external experts and academics to BrainTrust.

It was refreshing to see how the BrainTrust members embraced the idea that they were not approvers. They had to learn how to think like a startup when evaluating venture pitches. At one Brain-Trust meeting, the deputy Chief Financial Officer (CFO) pushed back when someone wanted to see a detailed five-year financial plan for a new venture. How often do we – finance people – support a proposal based on the potential of an idea, not detailed numbers?

The role of the SCVRC evolved. It was a single body charged with approving a venture's risk programme 'go-live' readiness, adopting or dispensing with policies, and monitoring risk within the Bank's framework. It operated like any other committee in the

Bank, with formal papers, minutes and individual accountability. Some of us were anxious that we were operating too much like the Bank, but, in hindsight, that was not such a bad thing.

The committee brought the right level of discipline as we matured from a startup to scale up. It infused a risk and governance mindset across ventures, most of whose leads had not operated a venture, and definitely not within a bank. Most importantly, it provided reassurance and credibility that we had appropriate governance measures in place. I only fully appreciated the importance of this last point the day when a Board member acknowledged how far we had come in making the Board comfortable with venture governance. This meant we could keep going.

MAKING GOVERNANCE FIT FOR PURPOSE

We were building ventures within a global bank. Banking is one of the most, if not *the* most, regulated sectors globally. Add to that the complexity of different regulators in different markets. With the exception of the two digital banks (Mox and Trust), no venture required a banking licence and many were financial technology companies or platforms. But given that most of them were 100 percent subsidiaries of the Bank to begin with, they had to follow all its policies and standards. As the Bank had numerous policies and hundreds of standards for subsidiaries, that was never going to work.

Ventures needed a risk-based approach that took into account the type of venture, and also its stage. I remember sitting through one committee discussion where members were debating whether it was okay for a venture to do beta testing with 10 banking staff members and whether they needed further permission and controls to test with another 50 members. On another occasion, a venture wanted to set up a landing page to gauge client interest in the idea, and prepared lengthy papers to support the idea, with which many departments had to get comfortable.

So, we went on a mission to design policies and standards that were fit for the purpose of the ventures. The project was aptly named 'Delta', and we got one of the big four names to help.

Nevertheless, the outcome of the first phase of Delta was that it did not meet initial expectations. We knew the project was complex and ambitious. We had to come up with something 'new' in only a few months, while the Bank had been at it for more than 150 years. The project did achieve the goal of moving the needle in some areas such as cloud governance, technology and information, and cyber-security standards. More importantly, it opened our eyes to what the Bank was grasping, and the magnitude of the challenge ahead of us. There were also some more lessons to learn.

First, over time, large organisations end up creating a process for everything imaginable. This may not be a bad thing for a large global organisation, but trying to untangle a small venture from that maze simply entangles it more. Why not design something completely new?

Second, people who have come from large organisations have lived those standards and processes for so long, that they have become over-reliant on them. They refer to processes to help them make decisions. Each process has multiple steps; each step has a different risk; each risk has a different owner. This is why most efforts to simplify will fail: we start from what we already have when what we need to do is to start from scratch. This is what startups and fintechs have shown us. It is not that people are not smart; it is that when they are in their role for too long, they get stuck in that mindset.

Third, the ultimate decision-makers are either hesitant or have no incentive to make things easier. If they are hired and incentivised for protecting the Bank, then why would they disrupt it? Whenever debates happened, whenever decisions were held up, I often heard people discussing whose 'neck was on the line'. Individuals alone are not responsible for this mindset; the regulated nature of the sector has a role as well.

We did not give up. We kept going and started Delta 2.0. This project was itself like a venture. You try, you fail, you pivot, and you keep going with multiple launches. This time we were counting on the Bank CEO, who had made both innovation and simplification his personal objectives. Deep down, he was frustrated that things were not moving quickly enough. This meant we could apply a more top-down approach, be radical and hold senior management to account.

DETACHING FROM THE MOTHERSHIP

We made it clear from the beginning that each venture would be set up as a separate legal entity. This was important for many reasons, but the main one was to ensure the venture teams get into the mindset early on, that they 'live and die' by the venture – not operate like a Bank project with a wide safety net. A separate legal structure also meant that the venture would be ready if and when we have partnership or investor discussions. The venture would have its own brand identity, could award equity stakes, and the Board was made accountable for decision-making.

The question was not about *if*, but *when*. Alex was adamant that we should set up legal entities early, for the reasons mentioned above. Yet, I wanted to make sure that ventures had validated the client proposition enough before we backed them to launch. Setting up legal entities was a huge resource commitment for the venture and added governance responsibilities. Most venture leads were not experienced entrepreneurs and, instead of focusing on the product and client, they were lost in entity set-up. And if the venture did not take off, we ran the risk of it winding down.

In hindsight, the delays in venture set-up did come back to bite us. When we hired external venture leads and let them incubate the venture for too long, it became difficult for that team to break away from the Bank. Teams started depending too much on the Bank's infrastructure and support, which limited their independence, which we wanted to encourage. We wanted ventures to come up with new ways of working. Bank salaries and venture salaries had to be different, both in quantum and in the mix, but that could only work when they were segregated. We later discovered that the delay also made the intellectual property (IP) transfers from the Bank to the venture time-consuming and complicated.

In the beginning, the idea of separate entities made everyone anxious. SOLV was the first venture to 'break away', but there were many questions, when people learnt they were in a different property, not connected to the Bank's network, with its own brand. We got better at it over time. We simplified the legal entity set-up process and created a standard set of systems, benefits and policies that could be replicated across ventures. In fact, this became our strength. Even when other business units wanted to venture out, they realised they needed our help with the set-up. It was not perfect, but we were the only unit to have successfully done it several times.

PEOPLE – THE BIGGEST ENABLERS

The single biggest driver of success for a venture is the venture lead and their team. A good leader and a strong team can successfully pivot an idea that may not look very promising on paper. But even a brilliant idea under a weak team may never see the light of day.

We learnt many lessons from dealing with a diverse set of individuals.

> *"A good leader and a strong team can successfully pivot an idea that may not look very promising on paper. But even a brilliant idea under a weak team may never see the light of day."*

While we backed a lot of internal talent to become intrapreneurs, in many cases they were not the right people to lead a venture. Pitching an idea and doing some background work is one thing; turning it into a full-fledged business is different entirely. We wanted to bring out the hidden entrepreneur. It did not take long to assess whether someone could build companies. As the venture ideas were related to financial services and were built from within the Bank, our ideal venture lead needed the traits of both an entrepreneur and a banker. Such a combination is difficult to find. Experienced entrepreneurs have 'been there, done that' and learnt from their failures. Internal candidates are familiar with banking and understand the pulse and dynamics of the organisation.

It is not all about the venture lead. The typical roles in a venture of a Chief Product Officer (CPO) and a Chief Technology Officer (CTO), from a delivery perspective, or a Chief Operating Officer

(COO) and a Chief Risk Officer (CRO), from a governance perspective, are important to get right. This is conventional wisdom and easier said than done. Typically, in startups, a team of co-founders come together and divides the roles and responsibilities. It is harder to inject that equation later.

Talent assessment is a continuous process. The skill sets and mindsets required for developing ideas, building and launching, and then scaling, are quite different. It is rare to find a venture lead or a team who can carry a venture through the whole life cycle. We started getting much better at assessing people who could take an idea from zero to one, then from one to ten, and from ten to a hundred. This meant asking people to step down or take a different role in the venture.

The role of a venture incubator became more important with time. Other labs call this role 'entrepreneur in residence' (EIR), but in a bank, it is a lot more. We defined the venture incubator simply as 'the co-founder without equity'. They had to handhold a few ventures until they were mature enough – guiding through strategy, proposition, partnerships, teams and funding. A key aspect of the incubator role was to help navigate a large organisation and unblock issues. For some high-conviction ideas, we assigned the most senior people as incubators.

WHY DO IT ALONE WHEN YOU CAN PARTNER?

One of the core beliefs at SC Ventures was to find the right partner at every stage of the venture. 'Partnership' is a broad term that, in our mind, included tech vendors, commercial partners, and strategic and financial investors. These collaborations taught us a couple of valuable lessons.

First, do not get carried away and become over-reliant on suppliers. We did not have a huge build machinery in-house and it was a non-starter to rely on the Bank's tech team, which operated at a different scale and cost level. So, venture teams were free to choose their own tech suppliers. We saw some early-stage ventures wanting to enter into equity share models to lock in the vendor or service provider and keep the costs low. While this sounds good in theory, most vendors are not set up for 'equity instead of services' and there are bound to be exclusivity and intellectual property (IP) issues. Ventures need to own the product and tech, make sure they have the right people, and be very selective on long-term equity partners who share your vision.

Second, the ventures should not underestimate the importance of commercial and strategic partners. Apart from funding and capabilities, a credible investor signals strong validation of the proposition and potential. For all the challenges associated with corporate ventures, the biggest advantage is access to the ecosystem of partners.

We were clear that these ventures would not remain 100 percent owned and funded by the Bank – that was by design. Even in the digital bank Mox, the Bank owned around 65 percent; for non-banking ventures, we were open to going below 50 percent. We saw a shift in mindset and financial commitment from the Bank, and interest from the external ecosystem each time a venture announced a strategic partnership. At the time of writing, examples would include investments from HK Telecom and PCCW, as well as C-trip in Mox, Northern Trust in Zodia Custody, and numerous other partnerships and yet-to-be-announced joint ventures.

It is not only about having the right investors. Having the right commercial or distribution partners makes a huge difference, both to the business case and the profile of the venture.

Traditionally, businesses had approached partnerships either for a product or for distribution. Over time, it became about creating and experimenting with business models together. It was not easy to find a like-minded partner, but when it worked, there was a tremendous upside.

REFLECTING ON THE PAST AND THE FUTURE

SC Ventures is a platform for innovation and business model experimentation with the mandate to create new options for banking. It is still too early to claim success, given the ventures are yet to reach the scale we want them to achieve. We know that, like any diverse portfolio, some ventures will eventually fail to reach their aspirations and may even wind down, but some will fulfil their promise and surprise us. As the Bank evolves in its journey to becoming future-ready, it would be gratifying to look back and say SC Ventures played a small part in it.

TAKEAWAYS

- You need to go into experimentation with an open mind – do not expect all the answers from the start, you can only learn by doing.
- Be prepared for a lot of challenges when you are building ventures – what will get you over the line is conviction, perseverance, a strong team and an ecosystem of partners.

17

CULTURAL PREROGATIVES: DIVERSE AND FLAT

Alex Manson

CEO, SC Ventures

"We had just taken away some of the crutches that people typically use to manage their careers: titles, reporting lines and systems."

Innovation almost always fails. There are several reasons why including entrenched interests, bureaucracy, and 'corporate antibodies' kicking into action. But when you set up an innovation lab or venture investment practice, are those in the mothership truly evil and hoping you will fail? Well, sometimes the answer feels like 'Yes'. But joking aside, obviously in reality the answer is 'No'. Something else is at work. We call it 'DNA'.

From our first day, we knew that transformation was not about technology but about business models, clients, ways of doing things, culture and mindset. In other words, it was about people.

FIGHTING COUNTERPRODUCTIVE HABITS WITH DIVERSITY

When SC Ventures took over the eXellerator, it already had a good reputation for helpful, creative people dedicated to the success of the organisation but for the eXellerator to genuinely have a transformational impact, the model had to change, along with the mix of people. We quickly hired a few bankers into it – from Transaction Banking, Retail, Financial Markets and other parts of the organisation – to create a diverse core team, to the point where it was uncomfortable to have everyone in the same room, as they came from such a multitude of backgrounds.

Most innovation labs are populated by highly creative people, who are well versed in design thinking, equipped with lean startup tools, and generally fond of technology and all things new. This creates an inspiring and energising environment, but one with little experience in running large businesses. So, there is a credibility gap when it comes to creating an impact in a larger organisation, let alone a regulated one like banking. Conversely, the problem with most corporate professionals is that, while some may think of themselves as innovative, the years spent in a corporation have conditioned them to do things in a certain way, which creates some counterproductive habits in an innovation context.

Corporations are meant to optimise for efficiency and mitigate risk, which is perfectly sensible when you know exactly what you are doing and where you are going: force accountability, eliminate duplication and kill distractions! Unfortunately, when you *do not* know where you are going, it makes little sense to go there efficiently. Here you want to solve for creation. This forces a manager to unlearn the ways they have managed their team and relearn how to create an environment for experimentation.

An example of counterproductive habits is dismissing ideas with phrases such as: "We tried that before. Here's what happened" and "This is a great idea, but X is already working on it. Why don't you guys talk and potentially join forces?" The former is a classic example of habits squashing innovation. While the latter starts out from a better place – wanting to avoid duplication and inefficiencies – but ultimately kills entrepreneurial spirit by suggesting that ideas are not that special, and anyone can run with them. Other examples include dwelling on five-year plans and budgets and measuring outputs (including profit and loss, and equity returns), instead of focusing on inputs (such as the quantity and quality of client interactions). They also include the very human need for control, which breeds micromanagement and risk or change aversion.

Cultural Prerogatives: Diverse and Flat 127

All these behaviours – conscious or subconscious, acquired or imposed – can be useful in stable circumstances, where the objective is to improve incrementally, extract efficiencies and sell marginally more of the same to marginally more people at marginally less cost. However, they are incompatible with innovation and the creative spirit that an organisation needs to unleash to reinvent itself.

Our challenge was how we should create a team that would address this dilemma, comprising smart, empowered and innovative people, yet possessing the credibility of bankers in a banking organisation.

A huge part of the answer is *diversity*: our eXellerator absorbed a diverse mix of people, to the point where it did get uncomfortable for all to be in the same room. This was exactly the intended effect. Our very first group meeting was loaded with apprehension. You could see the innovation folks regarding the bankers with suspicion and vice versa.

The point is that diversity is brutally hard! It forces people who normally would not want to hang out, to do work together, so it is deeply unpleasant at first. But once harnessed, that diversity is so powerful that a diverse team will invariably win over a less diverse one. Today, most corporations understand the importance of race and gender diversity; however, they have a hard time with a diversity of background, neurodiversity and the sort of character diversity I am describing here, because, in the absence of other guidelines, people still tend to hire and promote people like themselves.

At the scale of a large corporation, a critical element of diversity is the attitude towards growth and change. Are we hiring and promoting 'growth leaders', or are we hiring and promoting 'caretakers'? While these caretakers may well be good leaders and are typically diligent types who rise to senior management by doing a great job in a particular context, they do not create the true diversity needed for innovation. Caretakers want to protect or maintain the status quo, chain of command, or ways of working that are not conducive to reinvention. Such managers tend to tell people what to do because they have been conditioned to think that it is their job to be decisive. When they do this, they condition the people around them to expect to be told what to do, enforcing discipline but killing the intrapreneur spirit. These same managers also remove duplication and inefficiencies (inevitable by-products of innovation) and make few well-considered decisions once they have all the available information.

However, growth leaders' most important trait is admitting and being comfortable with the fact that they do not know much. Their job is not to tell people what to do, but to create an environment where people will figure this out for themselves. They are comfortable displaying gaps in knowledge and vulnerability to create a safe environment for others and to get the entire team's input and initiative in every circumstance.

Take a look at most companies' management teams, executive teams and boards. Even going two or three levels below, you will find a huge proportion of caretaker leaders. Do not get me wrong – they are hugely important. Businesses do require an element of administration and protection to mitigate risks. This is what caretaker managers do well while optimising processes. The point I wish to make is different: in the case of the SC Ventures core team, our secret was our diversity of traits and attitudes. We needed to force people on management teams to coexist and work collaboratively, even if they normally would not get along, because that is the result of such diversity. As long as managers hire managers like themselves, we lack diversity in the boardroom. This may be the single fact that invariably leaves established businesses vulnerable to external disruption at some point in time.

REPLACING HIERARCHY WITH A FLAT STRUCTURE

Over the years I had reflected on organisational charts and their roles in making a group or team successful. I found the following observations across different groups, specifically in the context of innovation:

Organisational charts get in the way of teamwork and, surprisingly, even accountability. Most staff escalate issues up multiple layers – to the bosses of their bosses – to avoid making decisions. And when that decision proves to have been wrong, it becomes incredibly hard to find who was the true culprit in that long chain.

Cultural Prerogatives: Diverse and Flat

Organisational charts and chains of command slow down information. The idea is that very few people make very few decisions once in possession of all the available information to ensure restraint and mitigate risk.

Business and functional silos do a terrible job of enabling cross-pollination, an essential part of the creative process. A creative environment needs to move information to as many people as fast as possible so that anyone at any level of the organisation can make fast decisions. This may well create inefficiencies, and perhaps increase risk, both of which are tolerated for the sake of truly empowering a team to figure out their next steps and actions by themselves.

The question was whether both mindsets, driven by fundamentally different organisational needs, were possible in the same corporation. The first step could well be that the mothership was organised in a certain way, with a regimented flow of information and chain of command, but the innovation lab or ventures were small and contained experiments on the side and therefore, organised in a different way.

PART OF THE BANK, BUT ORGANISED DIFFERENTLY

So, we experimented with different ways to organise ourselves: for a start, we avoided titles and organisational charts (an interesting journey for all and difficult for some). Instead, workstreams and tasks replaced organisational silos. People were assigned to workstreams – typically more than one – and those allocated to these workstreams reported to the workstream leads. When working on another workstream, they reported to someone else. Meanwhile, the leads were given individual accountability for their workstreams.

This approach took care of task-related performance management and accountability, but not overall performance management and coaching, which is the other task of a manager. To address this, we introduced performance coaches, later called 'Development Leads', for everyone in the team. Development Leads had to gather feedback from various workstream members, as well as from outside the team, to feed back to the members assigned to them in a constructive and growth-oriented way. This approach, while theoretically appealing, worked very differently for people as a function of the Development Leads themselves. We do not think we have mastered the skill and are still attempting to refine this model.

Aside from avoiding organisational charts, we also wanted to take a different approach to individual performance management. I had always disliked the conventional framework because of how it incentivised people to game the system, of the inauthentic conversations at the end of a year's worth of work ("I would have rated you a two instead of a three, but I was made to force-rank everyone"), and because of the artificial deadline of yearly objectives, which did not recognise changing circumstances.

We also took personal rankings out of the picture because most individuals react emotionally during grading and ranking, especially in any organisation using such rankings in the context of a limited remuneration pool. This distracts them from the real focus of a performance review, which should be more along the lines of: "On this task, you have done really well. Keep it up. But you have been terrible at that one. How can we help you? And by the way, let's talk about your career and your objectives in your professional life."

Existing systems could not always cope with the difference in approach. For a start, the Human Resources (HR) software needed a job title; a blank field was not allowed. To address this, and the flat organisational structure we wanted, we all entered the same title and became 'Members' of SC Ventures. The term stuck. Later down the line, we realised that while people liked being seen as 'Members', it was difficult to explain what they did. So, we asked Members to mention on their intranet profile what workstreams they were responsible for – for example, "I am responsible for this workstream. Talk to me about that project".

Second, the same HR system required reporting lines for administration such as expense approval and for regulatory purposes. To address this, all Members initially reported to the same Chief of Staff, though this soon created a bottleneck. We later distributed this administrative responsibility to different Workstream Leads. The idea was to separate the development and performance conversations from tasks, and objectives and key results (OKRs) management (more on that later).

Third, the HR framework called for well-defined titles or bands, dictating salary, progression, and access to certain jobs back in the corporation. It was challenging to build a framework that was somewhat separate from the Bank's, but that did not harm someone in the long run (such as transferring back to a business line or finding a job in another corporation, which would presumably be organised in a conventional way).

PERFORMANCE MANAGEMENT, BUT DIFFERENTLY

As it happened, one of the team members brought to work John Doerr's book, *Measure What Matters*, on OKRs. The notion of OKRs emanated from Silicon Valley and is widely used in the technology world.

OKRs are also a performance management tool, but differ from conventional corporate methods in significant ways:

- **They are aspirational, as opposed to 'do or die'.** It is expected that individuals may not achieve their OKRs, but the point is to set the bar high enough to achieve a lot.

- **They are typically set quarterly or more frequently,** instead of yearly objectives, reflecting a faster-changing environment that is more applicable to startups.

- **They are public for everyone in the team to see,** as opposed to a confidential conversation between a manager and an employee. This is both for the sake of transparency and to allow individuals to receive help from teammates in hitting their targets.

- **They are essential.** The question in determining the appropriate OKRs is: What is absolutely essential for the team to achieve in the context of surviving the next quarter? The answer to this question instantly clarifies priorities.

Initially, OKRs were associated with a lack of accountability. As to the lack of formal reporting lines, people tend to prefer clarity over ambiguity, which is human nature – and we had just taken away some of the crutches that people typically use to manage their own insecurity: titles, reporting lines and systems. We were at risk of designing a creative – but not very effective – chaos.

At a difficult 'admin team meeting' I remember hearing views on OKRs, flat structure, and organisational charts that did not say their names. I simply offered to revert to a conventional organisation: maybe we were not mature enough for the experiment. Maybe we had taken on more than we could chew. Most importantly, I was concerned that it was all getting in the way of being effective and enabling our mission.

A few people had advocated a more conventional organisational approach to give firmer accountability in our early days. To my surprise, a number of other members advocated against it, thinking we would be 'throwing the baby out with the bath water' and that it was special after all to be organised by outcomes rather than charts.

We all acknowledged that OKRs were not working, but we also realised we had tried to do everything very quickly, by ourselves, making it up as we went along. Honestly, what did we expect?! So, we decided to start this one again from scratch, and hired a consultant to help us avoid 'reinventing the wheel', but also avoid the traps of the system we were trying to implement. Twelve months later, OKRs had become really effective for us, and importantly were a *modus operandi* that the whole team said worked better for them. So, we had made progress.

DID WE MANAGE TO CREATE A 'SAFE SPACE'?

Not having titles does not imply there is no hierarchy. In a startup environment, hierarchy is typically present in the sense that the founder is in charge. But we did not really have a founder in that sense, as our mandate originated from the Bank. In fact, it was clear to us that it was CEO Bill Winters' support and endorsement that allowed us to exist in the first place, with a number of other senior supporters in business and functions.

Despite the lack of titles, a leadership structure quickly emerged, based on seniority and the nature of the tasks. We are still shying away from calling it a 'management team' and have resorted to the term 'admin group'; perhaps it was our attempt at maintaining the illusion of no hierarchy when one does exist.

A concept I like, and that I believe lays the foundation for a meritocratic environment, is the 'hierarchy of ideas' expounded by billionaire hedge fund manager Ray Dalio in his book *Principles for Dealing with the Changing World Order*. Dalio argued that anybody in an organisation should be able to prevail, irrespective of their rank, on the back of a superior idea. The question I had was how to make sure that I did not intimidate team members, especially the younger ones. I knew I could be forceful at times, so how would I convince everyone that pushing back, debating and raising controversial views really was okay?

I am guessing the answer is in the creation of a safe environment where individuals are not scared of the consequences of their words or actions, can think independently and also be themselves, focusing on work they love without needing to worry about what bosses or peers think of them. My assumption was that the flatter the hierarchy of the group, the more likely we would be to create such a safe space. At team meetings, I kept reminding the team that, of all the things they could do that would annoy me, telling me I was 'full of sh*t' was not one of them.

TAKEAWAYS

- The failure of innovation in an organisation is intrinsically linked to its cultural DNA – in other words, its people.
- Fighting counterproductive habits with diversity is brutally hard, especially with the competing attitudes of new 'growth leaders' vs traditionally minded 'caretakers'.
- Replacing hierarchy with a flat structure is a way of organising that part of the Bank differently, which affects many of the Bank's existing structures, systems and frameworks.
- Performance management measures, and issues of hierarchy both need to change to reflect the new culture in an organisation.

18

THE BIGGEST ENABLER: CULTURE

Gurdeep Singh Kohli

Operating Member

"When you are on a mission to rewire the DNA, the 'soft stuff' is indeed the hardest."

When I signed up for the mission to rewire the DNA in banking, I also signed up to rewire myself. I had been a strategy professional for over 15 years before joining SC Ventures. Like many peers in this space, I was acutely aware that strategy alone was not sufficient to succeed in the real world. One had to go deep into execution, make decisions and learn from mistakes, to understand what it takes to build businesses. SC Ventures was the best platform I could have asked for to make this transition.

During my strategy days, we often heard from business stakeholders, that while the plan might look good on paper, executing and getting things done was hard. I honestly used to think this was a lame excuse – and a result of poor leadership. How hard can it be to get things done, when the why, what, who are so clear? I have no hesitation in admitting that I was wrong. Setting up the first venture was a sobering experience. I am not suggesting that it gets easier the second time. The challenges of new businesses are so different, and it may even feel harder as you scale.

I reflected on what was the biggest impediment to 'simpler, faster, better' – something the Bank aspired to. It boiled down to one thing: culture. When you are on a mission to rewire the DNA, the 'soft stuff' is indeed the hardest. There are so many dimensions to culture. I am not referring to culture in the broader context of the organisation – we had well-defined valued behaviours in the Bank, which resonated with me personally i.e., *Better Together*, *Do the Right Thing*, *Never Settle*. I have always paid attention to what aspects of the culture get in the way of innovation.

ENCOURAGING SMALL EXPERIMENTS – START, FAIL, PIVOT, REPEAT

As organisations grow in size, they get more comfortable with multi-year projects with big budgets and over time, this becomes the norm. People need to be convinced, or shall I say need to promise, that these projects will be highly impactful. That they have thought through every aspect of the project in terms of costs, timelines, technology and adoption. That is the only way to get the project funded. This may work for investments that are mandatory and foundational. But innovation and experimentation go hand in hand – it is extremely challenging to project how it will pan out in financial or non-financial terms, even before you start.

It was not just with business models, anything we did to promote the culture of innovation through intrapreneurship programmes or proof of concepts with fintech partners, started with small experiments. This may sound so intuitive but trust me, this muscle needs to be trained, and should be an explicit part of the culture. It prevents people from analysis paralysis, from relying on perfect information to make the decision to move forward. It absolutely does not mean that you jump into experiments without any groundwork, but beyond a point, the only way to test whether the idea will work, is by doing. Almost certainly, it will fail the first time, forcing you to go back to the drawing board or pivot and start again. Which is why the experiments need to be contained, small in terms of time and money, so you can do multiple iterations. It did make many people uncomfortable when we pushed

The Biggest Enabler: Culture 137

to get things started with so many questions unanswered, and even more uncomfortable when the experiment failed and we said, "Let's do this again!"

CHALLENGING THE (DIS)COMFORT OF COLLECTIVE DECISIONS

I mentioned earlier that *good* governance does not mean *more* governance. Committees are a powerful governance mechanism when properly set up and managed. They bring diversity of views, help to check group thinking and serve as an engagement forum – all of which are valuable. While committees are needed in large, regulated institutions, it may become an impediment when experimenting, pivoting quickly, and encouraging individual accountability. More often than not, there are limited consequences for a person who sits on a decision, but there are adverse ones if they choose wrongly with imperfect information, which increases reliance on committees and paperwork.

Building an innovation culture needs different governance model that is fit for purpose. We paid attention to the number and constitution of committees in SC Ventures. More importantly, we empowered people to be individually accountable and to use their judgement. That did not mean they should not seek expert views; it simply meant we did not need 10 people to agree on every decision in writing. When flying a plane and there is trouble at 30,000 feet, only the pilots are responsible for making decisions at that moment. They should get help from the control tower, but there is no time to shop for opinions.

TACKLING THE BIGGEST UNSEEN BLOCKER – FEAR

Fear is a natural emotion. Courage is not the absence of fear but the ability to overcome fear. Look closely at successful, visionary leaders or transformative organisations, and you will find an abundance of courage. Rather than tackling fear itself, focus needs to be on instilling the confidence in teams to push the boundaries. To be clear, pushing the boundaries does not include misconduct or breaking the law; some boundaries should never be crossed and there should be zero tolerance in these cases.

So, what drives fear? At the heart of it is the fear of losing your job and reputation if you are fired. If the risk of losing your job because you have demonstrated courage, pushed the boundaries, or challenged the status quo, is a lot higher than being laid off, because you have kept your head down and delivered the results your boss expected, why would anyone push the boundaries? One may say: what's wrong with the latter? And I would say: nothing, if you were not serious about innovation and transformation in the first place. Keep calm and carry on.

People coming with years of experience in large organisations have a collection of stories when things went wrong. The response, many a time, resulted in more processes, controls and committees. And this becomes part of the muscle memory, ingrained in the DNA. Given new business building has its fair share of surprises and dealing with the unknown, it was bound to make people concerned, and think of what could go wrong, not necessarily based on facts, but based on past experience.

When you are innovating and experimenting, taking measured risks at each stage is a given. The challenge is how to make the risk mindset 'fit for purpose', so that everyone feels accountable for overall commercial success rather than risk operating in silos. Part of that was to encourage teams to lead with a solution, not the problem. Bill used to ask in town halls "How many of you are responsible for clients?" He would then stress that *every person in the room* was responsible for clients; that *everyone* was part of the business. By the same logic, embedding risk discipline in the minds of teams early on, prevents massive course correction later. It is easier said than done to be honest, but having tools, like objectives and key results (OKRs) and a common scorecard does help.

TAKING THE LITMUS TEST – WHAT HAPPENS WHEN THINGS GO WRONG

It is fashionable to use the innovation catchphrase 'learn fast, fail fast', but putting this into practice is a different ball game. Not the learning fast bit – but the failing bit.

The Biggest Enabler: Culture

Organisations can either feed fear or boost courage, depending upon the response to a mini-crisis or a period of turbulence. Leaders and managers need to be mindful that they focus first on solving the problem at hand, genuinely learning from it, and not on who made the decision, what should be the consequences and what new processes need to be put in place. Such a response can completely demoralise the team, and if it happens to anyone once, it is stored in his/her DNA.

If we do not check this, after a point, people stop making decisions; they rely on the process to make decisions for them. Daily life becomes process management – from hiring someone to getting a piece of software, expensing a claim, onboarding a vendor – you name it. How often have we heard someone who wants to take an initiative, check themselves by asking: But, what's the process?

I should stress that having a process is not a bad thing in itself. You need a process when you have reached scale, want to drive consistency, and get your message across to thousands of people. But letting it take over from judgement does not sit well with innovation culture. Worse still, taking a heavy-handed approach when someone does not follow a process or makes a poor judgement call can kill the entrepreneurial spirit completely. When an employee's judgement call becomes Judgement Day, it puts that person back in the box and the fear mindset becomes irreversible.

Over time, we have had our share of failures, and we know we will continue to have failed experiments as long as we are in this business. We have, consciously and collectively as leaders, come together in moments of crisis. The first and foremost priority is to ensure the problem is solved and that clients' interests are protected. We do reflect on lessons learnt and what do we need to put in place, but not with the intention to stifle experimentation, but to increase the probability of success.

BEING AWARE OF THE 'NOT INVENTED HERE' SYNDROME

One of the valued behaviours in the Bank is *Better Together*, and it encourages everyone to ask a simple question: How can I help? I find this extremely relevant when anyone in the organisation is attempting to walk the path less travelled. That individual should receive all the help he/she can get.

Sometimes that person faces discouragement: "We tried this before, it will not work"; or worse, faces hostility because of what we call 'not invented here' syndrome. This could be from within the team or even from the external parties. It is not that people have bad intentions when they do not engage – they may be quietly asking themselves: What's in it for me? If alignment with strategy and priorities is clearer and there is top-down support, things may fall in place naturally. But generally speaking, taking people along is harder, especially if you are tackling insecurity, ego or fear. You cannot force people to come with you or help you – you can either motivate them, request them or reward them. From a cultural perspective, it is important to try all of it.

I remember when we started making announcements when ventures or intrapreneur programmes reached milestones, I asked our marketing team to ensure we are acknowledging, or tagging the leaders who made it happen. Another example is that we were struggling to get traction from coverage teams to make client introductions – and it was quite obvious that we needed to not just request but find a way to reward their contributions. Even simple things like using the Bank-wide tool 'Appreciate' to acknowledge each other were important. These are not sure-shot ways to address this syndrome, but if you just wish it away, or bulldoze your way through, you will certainly fail.

DEFINING CULTURAL ATTRIBUTES – SO WHAT DID WE DO

Reflecting on our experience, and behaviours of both teams in SC Ventures and the Bank, we decided to define some valued behaviours for SC Ventures (in addition to what we had in the Bank). These were *Open, Challenging* and *Outcome Focused*. We even defined key words to make sure people understand what we expect from these behaviours, and what it is not.

Being *Open* is about respecting others' views, communicating willingly, helping others succeed, and promoting diversity.

The Biggest Enabler: Culture   141

Being *Challenging* is about experimenting, showing resilience, balancing judgement with risk, and not taking risks without thinking through the implications. Being *Outcome Focused* is to have an execution mindset, being accountable and not blindly delivering, only focusing on the outcome and not considering the approach or learning. It is one thing to have words on a slide, but embedding, living these values and changing the DNA takes longer. We have regular discussions on culture and even made these valued behaviours part of our people forum discussions and candidate assessment for new hires.

Did we manage to have an impact on the overall culture of the Bank? At the outset, the valued behaviours of the Bank are very well articulated, so there was no need to change anything. The objective was to just influence the innovation culture, which SC Ventures has been able to do, as evidenced by thousands of employees who have responded to the intrapreneur challenges, how we are applying OKR discipline across projects, the focus on simplification of processes, etc. Even external partners are looking at us for ideas on how they should embed transformational and innovation culture in their organisations. We continue to share our lessons and carry on our journey – let us not forget, culture is something we need to keep working on.

TAKEAWAYS

- Watch out for the cultural barriers to innovation and define what are the attributes you need from your team.
- Just like innovation, you will need to experiment and pivot a few times to address the barriers and promote the culture that will rewire the DNA.

19

AUTUMN

Michael Kruger[a] and Mark Dymock[b]

[a]*Previous CEO, Autumn*
[b]*Operating Lead*

Autumn is an open digital platform empowering clients across their retirement journeys. Key features include financial aggregation, wealth advisory, health-tech and other adjacent needs.

> *"You need to demonstrate as soon as possible that what you're doing is meaningfully different from business-as-usual — that it's not just innovation theatre …"*

Autumn's mission: To help everyone plan, manage and enjoy their retirement. Our mobile app provides independent, customer-centric tools, education, recommendations, insights, services and products across the aspects of wealth, and health. We provide financial clarity, helping users to create their personalised future and enjoy peace of mind today.

The world is full of uncertainty: global warming, viral pandemic, political instability, and market craziness. People are living for longer, the cost of living is increasing, and reliable market returns are becoming harder to find. In the face of all this, it is more important than ever to plan for the future. The year 2020 pushed us to reflect on what life is really about, and to consider what brings us joy and how we are going to pay for it.

Creating a future of purpose and joy requires planning – it is not going to happen by accident. And the sooner we start, the more likely we will be to achieve our goals. Despite this, planning for retirement seems to be universally difficult – almost one in two people fail to do anything about it before the age of 40. If you just heaved a huge sigh of relief on reading this, take heart – you are not alone.

There is a huge opportunity to help millions of people to create better retirement plans. Everyone wants to retire well, and financial planning is the natural wheelhouse of banks, *so: why aren't financial institutions already helping every single customer prepare for retirement?*

Challenge No.1: Providing financial advice is unprofitable – for most customers.

Challenge No.2: Motivating someone to act on their retirement plan requires *coaching*.

Challenge No.3: Poor financial literacy creates uncertainty and indecision.

Challenge No.4: Retirement planning *must* include health and lifestyle considerations.

Challenge No.5: Customers tell us that while they trust banks to *hold* their wealth, they do not necessarily trust them to *advise* on their wealth.

Challenge No.6: A side effect of banks losing the trust of their customers is that customers now bank with multiple institutions. This means that no single bank has a complete view of a customer's wealth, and advice based on a limited view is of limited value.

AUTUMN'S APPROACH

Given these challenges, we have crafted what we think will be a sustainable business model that addresses each of them.

Autumn:

- is affordable for all, by being digital-first and having marginal costs.

- uses gamification to coach people through, and over their emotional resistances.

Autumn

- provides financial education to improve literacy and build confidence.
- incorporates wearable and health app data to predict likely health costs due to lifestyle choices.
- builds trust using transparency and independence, and by being separate from the Bank.
- uses a subscription fee model instead of assets under management (AUM) to avoid misalignment of financial incentives.
- provides an open marketplace to avoid biased recommendations.
- has a business model that complements banks instead of competing with them, so users can manage all their finances and retirement plans in a single app.

I hope this provides a sense of the challenges we are facing, and of our approach to solving them. Now let us talk about building Autumn.

WHY CORPORATE VENTURE CAPITAL?

Building a sustainable fintech is hard. Customers have a way of stubbornly refusing to spend enough money to justify the initial acquisition costs, which for fintechs can run to hundreds of dollars per customer. Having a million pre-existing bank customers ready to register for your shiny new app without those boring marketing costs is quite attractive. Rapid scaling, and at a fraction of the usual customer acquisition cost (CAC) – what is not to love?

With that huge customer base comes an enormous amount of organisational expertise in terms of what problems those customers face, what solutions have been tried in the past, and what the most promising approaches are today. It is a treasure trove of hard-won information for the aspiring innovator.

Building a fintech requires hiring lots of weird and wonderful roles to deliver on regulatory matters, and this needs funding. Bank corporate venture capitalists are willing to support early-stage fintechs; they understand why all these people are necessary, and they even have some of them available on loan if you ask nicely – that is the magic trifecta of quality, speed and cost.

Given all that, you would *think* that building a fintech inside a bank should be easier. Instead, there is a different set of challenges. Substitute funding worries for concerns about stakeholder management, processes, approvals, and different rate of delivery, and then apply Hofstadter's Law (*"It always takes longer than you expect, even when you take into account Hofstadter's Law"*).

Luckily, SC Ventures is set up to be nimbler than the main institution. It has an extended support team to provide coaching, expertise, professional services, advice, governance, bank connections, external connections, camaraderie and even motivation. Think of them as a bank process strike force and cheer squad, but with agile sticky notes.

We have not yet achieved innovation nirvana, but we are getting better every day. However, the test is ultimately about creating sustainable businesses, so Autumn is very excited to be going live with our commercial offering.

SOME HOME TRUTHS FOR THE ASPIRING INNOVATOR

Lesson No.1: You are not a hero

Ventures need the support of the Bank to succeed, but the fastest way to kill support is to go in with the idea that "We are here to save the day!" Despite ventures being the means of exploring future business models, business as usual is the *business of today* and banks struggle to adapt to the innovator's usual rah-rah pitch and enthusiasm. It is important to be confident but *humble* if you want to build support. Learning from and building on the Bank's knowledge and experience of dealing with customers every day, is vital to the success of your venture.

Business as usual (BAU) is rightly sceptical about innovation kabuki, and this extends to being suspicious that the reason partners are dealing with your venture is only that they want more business with the Bank. Despite what partners say up-front, this is not always the case. When dealing with external partners, you cannot stress enough that your venture is independent and that you are not simply a back door into the Bank's customer base.

In tension with staying humble, you need to be confident and strong: building a venture in a bank means facing internal roadblocks as well as the usual external ones. You need to demonstrate as soon as possible that what you are doing is meaningfully different from BAU, that it is not innovation theatre, that you are exploring a sustainable business model as efficiently as possible, and that you are doing it in a way that is bank compliant.

Lesson No. 2: Risk has the power of veto, but zero risk tolerance means zero customers, so make them your partners

Risk exists for a reason and needs to be respected – regulation is not flexible. An important approach to launching your product is to get your risk colleagues familiar with your activities and decision-making processes. Start sharing early and help them incorporate into their own decision-making.

Early on in Autumn's journey, while we were still being encouraged by those in SC Ventures to be energetically entrepreneurial, I decided to conduct some market testing on our early proposition. Testing your ideas with real customers is the best way to find out what people really think, and it is the most fun part of the 'lean startup' process.

I decided to conduct the research myself, so over the course of an afternoon I registered some domains, created a landing page complete with some fairly anodyne text, a survey, and a form where users could register their interest, and I kicked the whole thing off with a small search engine optimisation (SEO) campaign.

Over the next week, a small team of people from Legal, Risk, Compliance, Marketing, Technology and Brand were in touch. Each, in turn, delivered a stern warning that I was breaching the process and advised me to stop and hand everything over. We turned the landing page off until Autumn submitted a paper seeking approvals from all concerned.

Submitting a paper for approvals is not always the answer. It took Autumn the better part of a year to convince those concerned that, as a non-banking app that conducts no financial transactions, it did not make sense to require Autumn to conduct Know Your Customer (KYC) for each of our users. While Autumn was learning and trying new things, the Process Owners were also having to do so.

The risk-based approach is anathema to credos, but it is non-negotiable for bank-owned subsidiaries. Being risk-based does not mean there is *no* risk at all; it means that you understand, quantify and manage it. The sooner you understand, embrace and extend to create your own risk framework, team and processes, the faster you will get to launch.

Lesson No.3: Respect and own your processes as soon as possible and secure the support of everyone involved until then

Every bank-owned entity is required to comply with its standards and policies, which means that unless and until Autumn creates its own processes that meet the compliance requirements *and* it has delegated authority from leadership in the Bank, Autumn would not be able to get going on its growth trajectory.

Heavy process means importing lots of Bank overheads right from the beginning – just when the startup most needs to be nimble. Non-compliance with regulatory requirements is not an option, so you need to respect and own your processes as soon as possible, to save wasting years on processes that have been designed for a bank and not a startup.

Lean startups are about *innovating to achieve results quickly and cost-effectively*. But for banks, *the process IS the result*. Innovators need to understand and respect the reasons why this is so, and find ways to comply as efficiently as possible, while creating their own infrastructure in parallel, so they can start personalising processes to fit their venture.

Autumn   149

The bottom line: the Bank is set up to optimise in its deeply embedded ecosystem. It is *now* learning to adapt to the weird and wonderful innovators. The Bank is bigger, and its processes will *crush* you if you do not have the support of the organisation – from the group CEO to Bob in Expenses, and the latter is harder to win over than the former. Make sure you know you have that organisational support – including aligned key performance indicators (KPIs) and incentives – well before you start anything.

Autumn is not yet large enough to have its own teams for functions such as Industrial Control Systems, Supply Chain Management, Compliance and Legal, so we are reliant on the SC Ventures' teams to support this. We are eternally grateful for the patience and support of our colleagues in the Bank – any successes we garner are underpinned by their hard work.

Although building a venture within a bank is a completely different adventure from the journey of an independent startup – the big family comes with surprising challenges and pressures – it also comes with many benefits.

With a bit of luck, Autumn will become *the* retirement planning and management platform, and we will help millions of people create and enjoy meaningful, purposeful and happy futures. And when we do, it will be because Autumn has grown from, and been supported by everyone in Standard Chartered Bank – a company that is truly *Here for Good*.

TAKEAWAYS

- Do not be a hero – stay humble and understand that processes are there for a reason.
- Risk has power of veto, so make them your partners.
- Respect and own your processes as soon as possible and secure the support of everyone involved.

EPILOGUE: WHERE DO WE STAND IN 2024

Mark Dymock – Operating Lead (interim CEO of Autumn, 2023-2024)

Autumn's business model, team and focus have been through multiple changes since this was written. The Autum technology platform is now part of a joint venture between SC Ventures and Next176, the venture arm of Old Mutual of South Africa, called Vault22. Vault22's mission remains that of Autumn – democratizing financial planning and giving people the ability to take control of their financial future – but with a slightly narrower scope ('health and wealth' turned out to be a difficult customer proposition) and a different geographic focus (Africa and the Middle East).

Re-reading Mike's chapter above some time later leads to a few reflections:

- First, that the original ambition for Autumn very much remains valid – the market has yet to deliver digital financial advice for the mass-market, and the great majority of the world's population is not getting something they would hugely benefit from.

- Autumn was one of the earliest ventures, and the first venture that sought to deal directly with individual clients as a regulated entity; as such, it was somewhat of a guinea pig for SC Ventures' risk and control functions. It is pleasing to be able to say that processes – and more importantly the sense of partnership – have evolved significantly since then.

The approval process for a new venture is now significantly more streamlined. Indeed, it is now clear there has been huge value in the SC Ventures functions bringing these learnings back to their colleagues in the 'mothership'.

20

THE ROLE OF TECHNOLOGY IN SC VENTURES

Michael Gorriz

Previous Head of Technology Transformation Organisation,
Standard Chartered Bank

"The operating model defines the character of the employees."

It should come as no surprise that all of our ventures need technology, and for some of them, technology is even a differentiating factor. Speed is paramount for producing the Minimum Viable Product (MVP), but at the same time, the solution needs to be scalable in case the MVP is successful. In most cases, the team has to build the solution from scratch because the Bank's existing systems cannot be used for the ventures. So, you need to define requirements, establish the right architecture and design, and quickly ramp up the implementation team. This all requires technology leadership. In technology-driven ventures, the founder is usually a top technologist who is then able to attract top technical talent who have vision and passion. On the other hand, when technology is a necessary but not a sufficient factor, it is harder to attract the talent you need. SC Ventures' BrainTrust often asks the question: "Who is your Chief Technology Officer (CTO)?" Quite often the answers range from helpless to desperate.

In search of a solution, many heads then turn to the Chief Information Officer (CIO) and ask whether corporate tech, with its deep pool of resources, could help: "Surely you can find a few capable people who could help us build a quick solution?" To respond to this request, we need to look at the role of corporate IT.

An IT landscape of a large corporation has to support the existing business end-to-end. This covers the customer channels over the many, complex workflows to solid record systems that keep all the data with the utmost security and continuity. The team has to maximise the service uptime, run the system at an optimal – mostly at a minimal – cost, and allow the flexibility to accommodate new requirements in a reasonable time and at a reasonable cost. If you are in a regulated industry such as banking, you need to comply with all the regulations. The weighting varies according to the situation of the enterprise, but typically you have an emphasis on compliance and stability, followed by cost and, lastly, flexibility.

This defines the way you work. The response to regulation comes along with a lot of procedures, elaborate risk management frameworks and a certain bureaucracy, to ensure you are always able to prove your formal compliance. Recently, the need for cyber-resilience has grown exponentially. In large corporations, this has led to even tighter guidelines, given the many potential vulnerabilities driven by the sheer size of the organisations and their unavoidable legacy.

To guarantee stability, there is a tight regime for introducing change, with stringent approval processes and clear accountability. Production changes are tested and vetted by a variety of people to ensure there is no adverse impact on the ongoing services. To keep costs under control, assets are often used by many teams. Shared infrastructure is common, and systems are used across countries and functions where appropriate. Changes naturally involve a broad spectrum of systems, and integration requires the attention of multiple teams. The co-ordination is often more laborious than the change itself, which leads to a significant lead time. None of this is bad in and of itself, or intentional; rather, it is the consequence of the chosen priorities of the four main key performance indicators (KPIs): compliance, system uptime, cost to serve and flexibility to change.

The Role of Technology in SC Ventures

Given the fact that the big motherships are also living in a world of volatility, uncertainty, complexity and ambiguity (VUCA), we see a slow shift towards more flexibility and an even higher uptime due to digital requirements, at the expense of increased cost. But these shifts are rather tectonic, due to the size of the organisations and their chosen architectural patterns.

In a venture, the four main KPIs are sorted in reverse. Flexibility is paramount to identifying the sweet spot of your offering. You need to be cautious with your investment, but there is little focus on the run cost up-front. Cyber-security and stability are table stakes when going live, but due to the absence of customers – and, hence, critical data – there is nothing to be protected up-front. Fast delivery cycles, outstanding user interface/user experience (UI/UX) and the ability to pivot in record time are the attributes that are initially sought. Features and functions are favoured over stability and maintainability. These priorities have a fundamental impact on the operating model, which in turn defines the character of the employees. A higher ratio of generalists and hands-on people is needed in ventures, while the overly diligent are less common. For this reason, a corporate IT department is not the first place to source, in droves, the technology talent that ventures need in their initial phases.

There are two possible avenues: 1) hire the necessary engineers from the market; or 2) employ service providers who are specialised in supporting startups. Whichever path you take, you have to ensure that the core team has the appropriate technical capability concerning architecture, design and operating model, as well as the necessary domain knowledge. Technology strategy and leadership cannot be sourced from third parties but is essential for any venture these days. Finding the right CTO is one of the first tasks in any venture and a condition for going forward. It can be the founder itself and they must be part of the inner circle.

The next step is to source the right talent to build the solution. Ideally, hiring the right people will give us the utmost flexibility by allocating dedicated resources to a project. If the required quality or quantity of talent is not available in-house, flexible outsourcing is the next best option. SC Ventures has developed relationships with many experienced service providers that can ramp up resources quickly and start designing and building the technical artefacts.

The Bank's IT department working on an arm's-length basis is one of these providers, especially when infrastructure services or special domain knowledge is needed.

Following these guidelines means a rapid start and the delivery of workable MVP. Unfortunately, it does not guarantee a fast market launch. As an example, Mox lost roughly nine months from the first MVP to the point of regulatory approval. Instead of the required risk management framework, which rules the cyber, technology and outsourcing procedures, the initial MVP did not satisfy the regulatory requirements stipulated. A period of onerous rework, documentation and testing was required to finally pass all the necessary tests to successfully launch the bank.

In the second banking-related venture – Standard Chartered nexus – we followed a different path. While the technology team building the solution was independent of the Bank's technology department, we applied the same controls and most of the procedures to build nexus. One reason for the decision was that nexus works on top of the Bank's systems and uses its licence to operate. Therefore, there was little room to manoeuvre, and the time needed from start to launch was considerably shorter. However, the path was not without friction. The application of the Bank's existing control framework often was – and still is – not fit for purpose for a fast-changing startup. Venture leadership often felt hampered by these controls, while the control owners also felt stretched to the point of feeling discomfort with the requests and expectations of the venture team.

TAKEAWAYS

- Talent to lead the startup technology might not come from within the company and you may need to look outside for the people you need.

- Even when you have a Minimum Viable Product (MVP), it can still take time to bring it to market if you cannot meet formal banking requirements.

- Traditional IT teams prioritise regulation over flexibility, and this is not well matched for startups.

21

MOX: A NEW, VIRTUAL BANK

Deniz Güven

Previous CEO, Mox

Mox is a digital bank that delivers a suite of retail banking services and lifestyle benefits all in one place, growing your money, your world and your possibilities.

> *"We are connecting banking into people's everyday lives and shaping a new model that just might reflect the future of banking."*

Mox in a nutshell: Mox is a virtual bank in Hong Kong, hosted by Standard Chartered in partnership with Hong Kong Telecom (HKT), PCCW and Trip.com. Launched in September 2020, Mox is now one of the fastest-growing and highest-rated retail banks in Hong Kong, with around 600,000 customers as of 3 July 2024, representing more than 10 percent of the bankable population in Hong Kong. Around one in five people under the age of 40 in Hong Kong are Mox customers, more than a quarter of the customer base uses four or more of its products. Mox boasted the top-rated virtual banking app on the App Store in Hong Kong (scored 4.8 out of 5) and the top Net Promoter Score (NPS) among all Hong Kong virtual banks. It represents a new generation of challenger banks; not simply a response to traditional banks, it offers a new operating model for banking that could be a forerunner of the future of banking. Mox has also been recognised by global management consulting firm Oliver Wyman as one of the fastest growing digital banks in the world.

Mox's landing page: mox.com

DRIVING THE EVOLUTION OF 'DIGITAL' IN BANKING

My journey, that led to the creation of Mox, started in banking, initially in Istanbul. In 2001, I took on my first 'digital' role at HSBC, but the concept of digital meant something quite different from what it means today. To most people at that time, 'banking' meant branches and ATMs. Online banking was still new and mobile banking did not even exist yet. At that time, we were exploring the potential of the internet to look at different ways to engage with customers, beyond the traditional branch network.

This same question: "How can we engage with customers in new ways, to create a new customer experience that hasn't been possible before?" has continued to dominate my career. I worked for several banks in different cities around the world: London, Hong Kong, Curitiba, Budapest, Kyiv, and Moscow. While the payment methods, banking systems and culture differed in each location, the aim was still the same: to reshape banking and make it easier, safer and a delight for customers.

When the financial crash hit in 2008, there was a universal loss of trust in banks. People were also changing how they bought products and interacted with banks. This led to a rise of digital 'challenger banks'. These were new, digital-first banks, such as Metro Bank, which launched in the UK in 2012, and our own digital bank, the first in Turkey, in 2013. It was an entirely different model of banking and customer engagement, with a team and technology infrastructure distinct from the rest of the Bank.

"This reflected an entirely different model of banking and customer engagement, with a team and technology infrastructure distinct from the rest of the Bank."

These experiences culminated in a move to Standard Chartered Bank in Singapore in 2017. Creating digital experiences and solutions in Asia is a very different proposition from trying to do so anywhere else in the world. Hong Kong, is where the Bank has the strongest franchise, followed by Singapore and South Korea, which have the highest rate of smartphone use in the world, with almost 90 percent of people aged ten and over, owning a phone. This unparalleled level of digitisation among the population means that expectations – and competition – are very high.

CREATING THE VISION OF VIRTUAL BANKING

In late 2017, the Hong Kong Monetary Authority (HKMA) announced its Smart Banking initiative. This comprised seven elements, one of which was to facilitate virtual banking in Hong Kong through virtual banking licences. Standard Chartered Bank looked at what this meant, and at what virtual banking could offer in Hong Kong that traditional banking could not or did not offer. The enormous opportunity this presented was clear, but our enthusiasm was not immediately shared more widely across the Bank. After all, we already had a banking licence in Hong Kong, so why would we need another?

We asked ourselves, and senior management, two things:

- Can we **defend** our market with our existing model?
- Can we **attack** this market with our existing model?

Far more than talking about virtual banking in conceptual terms, these questions resonated. We already had a fantastic global customer base, an extensive branch network, and a strong brand and presence. We offered a variety of existing digital capabilities. These strengths were not enough, however, to differentiate us or to create a new offer among an increasingly digital customer base. They would also not allow us to defend our market against challenger banks that entered the market on an entirely digital ticket. Based on these somewhat sobering reflections, we gained senior management support to explore the feasibility of a virtual licence. However, a 'Yes' does not necessarily mean that things move quickly.

One of the first questions we had to answer was: "What is a virtual bank?" In particular, we had to be clear that we were not simply developing a mobile app and a new marketing approach. For us, 'virtual banking' means building something from scratch: a new operating model, as well as a new technology stack, that could ultimately point the way to the future for Standard Chartered Bank.

The next big question was: "How much money would we need to develop it?" We had a meeting with senior management with no PowerPoint, no projector and no calculations. They asked how much money we needed, and it was impossible to give them an answer. I realised that we probably had one chance at this and that asking for money later would be far more difficult. But should we ask for US$2 million, $10 million, or $20 million? We went for US$60-65 million and got it approved. This whole process was a revelation to me. I had not fully appreciated before then that even a large, global bank can be agile and visionary. Rather than having to 'fight' for a share of the wallet, we could get it if we brought the right ideas, and the Bank shared our vision.

REALISING THE VIRTUAL BANKING CONCEPT

We started to build a team in Singapore, initially for research. We did detailed market research to understand the banking pain points for Hong Kong residents. Consultants sent us multiple documents, and we sourced a great deal of internal research from within the Bank.

We had lots of facts, but no insight. Several people told me that I would not fully understand the Hong Kong market unless I lived there. I realised that they were right. For example, the research illustrated that people may have, say, six cards in their wallets. But why? Cashback incentives may seem to be an obvious reason, but did that explain what people really want?

We reached out to 2,000 Hong Kong citizens and, as a result, uncovered 87 pain points in retail banking in Hong Kong, across onboarding, payments, channels, savings, and more. Some of these were major issues; some were irritations. Ultimately, this approach was essential to defining the journey that would ultimately lead to

Mox. We were clear that we wanted to be a service-led bank, not a product-led one. Service was essential to differentiate our offering in a mature market such as Hong Kong. Despite its advanced digital awareness and adoption, it had far less of a service culture than other markets.

For example, it typically takes two or three days – if you are lucky – to open a bank account in Hong Kong, despite being one of the most advanced banking markets in the world. The process requires a lot of documentation. It can be stressful and labour intensive for both customers and the bank. We wanted to completely reshape the way that customers engaged with the bank from the start, not simply to add a different coloured card to their wallets.

Customers should choose Mox as a lifestyle choice, not only as a banking choice. They should be able to open an account in minutes and receive a virtual card, ready to use, in real-time. They should also gain more from us than from banking services alone. For example, banks process an enormous amount of data, but the benefits of this data often only apply to the bank itself. We wanted to harness this data to give Mox customers useful information that they would not be able to source otherwise. For example, if someone travels by Uber every week to the same place, but on one occasion the price is higher even though traffic is not heavier than normal, we can alert them.

BUILDING A BANK

While thinking is easy, the building is far less so. We started to build an entirely new infrastructure for Mox in early 2018 with only seven or eight people and applied for a Hong Kong virtual banking licence shortly afterwards. The application process took around four months and was probably the most intense period of my life. There were so many elements to consider, many of which were completely new. Although I had been in banking for 20 years, I had never had to look at the entirety of a bank at once, from the first days of its origination right through to an exit strategy.

We worked with experts and visited the HKMA 16 times over that period. I will always remember the first of those meetings.

I could see by their faces that they thought that I, an unknown guy from Istanbul, was mad to entertain the idea of applying for a virtual banking licence in Hong Kong. After a couple of meetings, though, we started to build a rapport. I did not simply present solutions to them; instead, I outlined options, and tested digital banking models from India and the UK to discuss and get input on what they were looking for. This would be the first banking licence to be awarded in Hong Kong for over 20 years and the first-ever virtual bank licence. As a result, we were all learning through the process, and we learned a lot from each other.

The HKMA received 32 applications for virtual banking licences, including from major Chinese, US and UK players. It took time to review each one in detail, but we maintained our dialogue throughout. Then some of the other applicants started to approach us, including a major Hong Kong-based company looking for a joint venture and suggested working together. As our conversations continued, while other applications faded away, the number of approaches started to ramp up. We formed major partnerships with Hong Kong's telecom and lifestyle leader PCCW, and Asia's largest online travel agency, Trip.com.

Forming these alliances represented a major change in the development of Mox. I knew from my experience, as well as from all our research, that you cannot be successful in this industry if you work alone. You need partners to build an ecosystem and diversify distribution channels, particularly for service-led banks like Mox. We wanted Mox to become integral to people's lives, so working with partners that had already achieved this, to create joint service offerings, was key to our value proposition.

In March 2019, we were awarded the licence, one of only three such awards in this first phase. Far from being the end of the process, however, it was only the beginning. We had 46 people employed at that point and we started to build a bank. Over the next year, we ramped up recruitment, worked ludicrous hours, and our families forgot who we were. We started with an entirely 'blank page', rather than using any of the Bank's existing technology platforms. As a result, we would become one of the world's only cloud-native banks, a characteristic shared only by challenger banks.

Mox: A New, Virtual Bank   161

This made our development and our ultimate technology infrastructure cheaper, faster and more resilient.

Building a bank is an enormous undertaking. Although we did not use Standard Chartered Bank's technology, we took full advantage of the Bank's expertise, as well as engaged with several fintech providers. By harnessing the power of our entire ecosystem, we could accelerate development and source best-in-class capabilities, such as using machine learning (ML) to strengthen and streamline anti-money laundering (AML) compliance. Even so, creating robust regulatory compliance and risk modelling frameworks, together with security and scalability, is a major project. In this respect, most fintechs are fundamentally different from banks – in the language they speak, the way they operate, and the range of factors they need to consider. While we wanted to bring many of the advantages offered by our fintech partners, we are a bank and needed to fulfil the obligations of a bank.

NEW WAYS OF DRIVING AND MEASURING SUCCESS

Much of this innovation took place 'behind the scenes'. In reality, we wanted banking to be all but invisible to our customers, with as few points of friction as possible. This informed our key performance indicators (KPIs). For example, we set an onboarding target – that is, the time from account application to the activation of the card for use – of three minutes and 45 seconds. This approach is very different from more conventional banking KPIs, which generally focus on attracting new customers, revenue, deposits and profitability. To be a truly service-led bank, our KPIs needed to be based on the experience of people using our service. Without this approach, which is a very different mindset from traditional banking, we would end up with the same business model – with all its pros and cons – as any other bank. If we got the customer experience right, customers, revenue and profitability would ultimately follow.

Our differences in culture from a conventional bank were also reflected in our hiring culture. We have all fallen into the trap of hiring people who look, sound and think like us, but this makes it impossible to build something genuinely different. As a regulated business, it is tempting to think that innovation and agility are impossible in a bank. Everything we had experienced since we first went to senior management with the early Mox concept, right through to discussions with the HKMA and our ecosystem partners, showed me that this is not the case. Consequently, in seeking future employees, we had the confidence to look beyond education and professional background and to seek potential, attitude, and willingness to drive and embrace change.

Our marketing approach was also different. Marketing is very often defined, and its success is measured, in terms of TV adverts and social media campaigns. But while a catchy advert might lead to new customers, it does not help you measure the overall customer experience. Unless marketing is performance-based, it becomes primarily a branding exercise. Branding is important, but it should not be confused with marketing. We monitor our KPIs every day, using real-time intelligence.

WHAT ABOUT MOX?

However innovative our business and service model, however radical the shift towards numberless, virtual cards might be, and however satisfied our customers, the question we are asked most often is: "Why 'Mox'? What does it mean?" We modelled around 2,000 possible names, but many of these meant something in one language or another. We canvassed customers, and around 70 percent of them chose 'Mox'. It has many possible meanings, including 'mobile experience' and 'money experience', rather than one single meaning. It will evolve over time.

Choosing our brand colour – 'trust blue', as it is called – was also a departure from the norm. Many brands use red as their corporate colour, particularly in China. Our shade of blue is a mix between the Standard Chartered Bank blue and green, although this is not common knowledge or even all that interesting to most people. Our name, colour, branding, card and service offers are all distinctive, however; and every element of our identity plays a role in this differentiation.

REFLECTIONS UPON LAUNCH

It would be an understatement to say that 2019 was a tough year. We launched our alpha test in August of that year with a few internal users, moved to beta in December, and unveiled our name and brand in March 2020. We officially launched to everyone in Hong Kong in September 2020.

Our customers are of all ages, from 18 to over 80. They used Mox Card for everyday transactions as well as for high-ticket items. Customers have also enjoyed very fast and efficient account opening – the record is two minutes and 47 seconds.

Looking at the history of most banks, the speed with which we have reached this point is remarkable. We have fit years of evolution into barely more than two years, including applying for and receiving a banking licence. At times, particularly during the darkest and most difficult hours, it has felt like far longer. Just because we built a bank at pace did not mean we could take shortcuts or ignore our obligations to regulators, shareholders and customers.

I am often asked how I will measure the success of Mox. There are our service KPIs, as well as the expectations of our shareholders and stakeholders. Perhaps my father's reaction is the nearest I have come so far to know whether I have achieved what I set out to. In my 20 years of banking, I have never really been able to explain to him what I do: if I was not a branch manager, then what had I achieved in banking? Over the past two years, finally I have been able to explain – and he has understood – what I do, and why I am doing it. We are a company that builds trust. We are not a technology company; we are not a bank as many people would understand that term. We have built a new bank, based on trust and service. With the support of our partners, we are connecting banking to people's everyday lives and shaping a new model that just might reflect the future of banking.

Our goal is to win 'heart share', rather than market share. If we make ourselves more relevant to our customers and their daily lives, we believe the business will follow, not the other way around. We will do this by serving our customers with a whole new way of banking, by putting the power of banking literally in their hands. We aim to put the heart in banking and to win heart share. It is trust and a partnership that we want to build. When our customers grow, we will grow too.

TAKEAWAYS

- Mox was built to put customer experience ahead of any other goal – to win 'heart-share'.

- It was important to build the bank from scratch so it could have a new DNA.

- Building relationships with the right people and companies helped meet the requirements for the license but also launch in the right way.

22

CONTROL PREROGATIVES: GETTING THE GOVERNANCE RIGHT

Gwenda Phillips

Member, Risk Lead

"Taking risk ... isn't an option or a business model but is instead core to ... survival."

RIGHT SIZING THE MODEL

Ventures are defined as "a new activity, usually in business that involves risk or uncertainty; a risky or daring journey or undertaking". This means that, by their very nature, they are exposed to new risk. Ventures are supposed to be a journey into uncharted territory in search of value, where the prize is only available after risks are overcome. Indeed, much of humanity's scientific, technological and economic progress has been propelled by our ability to take risks. In fact, the world would be quite a different place if some of those risks had not been taken to push the boundaries of existing possibilities.

For the financial services industry, the adoption of technology and digitisation represented a watershed moment. Corporations risked losing any edge from their presence on the high street and jostling for space among the clutter of icons and apps on smartphones. In countries that are ahead in digital adoption, such as China, the struggle is even more intense, as the services offered by these corporations are reduced to another menu option on social networking, messaging and information-sharing apps such as WeChat.

If this is the future of financial services, then taking a risk, 'going' the digital or the fintech venture way, is not an option or a business model but is instead core to its survival. Yet, despite this, and despite having weathered innumerable storms, the largest and most successful financial services corporations struggle to achieve better success rates for their innovations than startups. A Harvard Business Review article in 2019 noted that the failure rate of innovation models in global companies remains an unflattering 70-90 percent.

SO, WHY ARE LARGE MULTINATIONAL CORPORATIONS, WITH AN ABUNDANCE OF TALENTED AND DEDICATED PROFESSIONALS, UNABLE TO DO MUCH BETTER THAN THE 'GARAGE' STARTUPS?

Some of the challenges we identified that impact a corporation's ability to succeed include:

Failure to recognise each other's biases: Institutional memory can become the hallmark of a large corporation's activities and inadvertently create blind spots. Conversely, new entrants may not have had the experience to identify risks that those who have been in a large organisation can foresee. The key is recognising that we each have our inherent blind spots.

Inability to scale flexible, risk-based approaches: Given large corporations' predilection to build fail-safe and consistent approaches, their ability to see risk-based approaches that can flex and be strong enough to meet the needs of multiple parties (ventures, the wider corporation and regulators) can often be constrained to process-led improvements, rather than definitive new principal-led models.

Control Prerogatives: Getting the Governance Right

Low incentives for Business and Risk teams to co-operate with adequate independence: In a system of checks and balances strongly based on separation and independence, an appropriate level of collaboration of Business and Risk teams can become an anathema.

Maintaining the status quo: This often arises from a human desire to maintain what we know and trust, including the methods, governance structures and reporting lines that underpin them – even if these could be fundamentally changed to compete effectively with the outside world.

HOW DID WE BUILD AN INNOVATIVE APPROACH TO RISK AND COMPLIANCE FOR VENTURES THAT PRIORITISES FREEDOM AND GROWTH WHILE ALSO CREATING CONTROL AND THE ABILITY TO PIVOT?

We worked together and assumed the best intentions of our peers when co-creating new approaches. We found that we had the most impact and accountability when the Business, Risk and Governance teams from both the ventures and the wider corporation (i.e., the head office) co-developed approaches, policies and risk software for the venture together. This type of collaboration had each other's interests at the forefront. However, for this approach to operate effectively we needed to make sure we worked with the right stakeholders within these teams. Stakeholders that had insight into the venture and what might be around the corner. Without this knowledge and their accountability, the risk approach could become meaningless.

HOW DO YOU DESIGN TOOLS FOR SPEED?

Racing a Formula One car requires a different level of control than taking the family car to the supermarket. Similarly, the frameworks, policies and tools built for scalable, efficient and highly regulated corporations do not necessarily make sense for a five-to-twenty-person business with a lower risk level. This does not mean that these frameworks are not vital to success, but that they need to be purposefully built. This is no simple task. Over the past years, we have spent – and continue to spend – time challenging and revising our existing policies, procedures and tools so that they are clear, simple and appropriate for the size and nature of the venture. This takes time but it is worth it. We have seen first-hand how a strong right-sized risk programme can add direct value to our ventures in the kind of external investment they attract.

HOW DO YOU ENABLE STRONG CO-OPERATION WITH ADEQUATE INDEPENDENCE?

The ability to co-operate and simultaneously have independence was perhaps one of the toughest and most important challenges facing the Business and Risk teams. If these teams' end goals are not aligned, it will be nearly impossible to succeed.

We can illustrate how this can work by looking at a relay race. In this kind of race, all of the team's runners are running independently, but they all have the same goal. The team needs independence to play to the strengths of each runner, allowing them to focus on their leg, rather than the race as a whole. In venture building, this is similar to having the Business and Risk teams each focus on their respective strengths. Although both teams have the same goal – namely, a successful venture – they each have different parts to play in achieving that goal.

What can make or break it for a venture is when the baton changes hands. It is this moment that dictates whether the entire race can be won or lost. In ventures, the baton is the information that needs to be shared between the Business and Risk teams. Reducing the friction in these handovers is paramount to achieving success.

IF A CORPORATE VENTURE WANTS TO GO AS FAST AS IT POSSIBLY CAN, AS SAFELY AS POSSIBLE, WHAT DO YOU NEED?

Answer: Business, Risk, Governance, Ventures and head office working together in the 'pit' to co-create effective risk and governance programmes that allow the venture to accelerate at speed in a controlled manner, and to drive up enterprise value.

Control Prerogatives: Getting the Governance Right   169

When the Business team engages Risk right from the beginning, and then along the journey at each key milestone, the process of analysing and managing the risk and governance for a venture becomes faster, smoother and more efficient. Importantly, this level of co-operation does not get in the way of independence but allows for greater transparency, safety and speed.

Co-operation with independence can be achieved.

TAKEAWAYS

- Collaboration with Risk teams is essential to the success of a venture.
- Running these seemingly opposing teams together is much like running a relay race – each has the same goal but needs to focus on their leg of the race and ensure smooth transitions of data and information flows.
- The earlier that right-sized risk programmes are embedded, the more value they can add for investors.

23

ZODIA: RETHINKING THE ROLE OF BANKS IN THE CRYPTO REVOLUTION

Maxime de Guillebon

Previous CEO, Zodia Custody

Zodia Custody is a crypto asset custodian that truly understands custody and enables institutional investors to safely and securely participate in the future of investing.

> *"Cryptocurrencies could become a legitimate and potentially exciting mainstream asset class and a way to hold value, as well as a means to conduct transactions."*

Zodia in a nutshell: A new crypto-custody service that offers institutional clients, including fund and asset managers, the ability to present a new asset class to investors, but with the assurance of a bank custodian.

THE CRYPTO REVOLUTION

Cryptocurrencies have been in the news since the birth of Bitcoin in 2009. In the decade since, more than 6,000 have been created. The headlines are rarely positive with a widespread suspicion that cryptocurrencies exist only for drugs, arms, money laundering and trading on the dark web. While these criticisms are often fair, it does not necessarily follow that because they are used for illicit purposes (as indeed, every currency is), cryptocurrencies are in themselves fundamentally evil.

As a bank, and as a team within the Bank, Standard Chartered was as influenced by the negative press as any other institution. After all, why would a bank align itself with – or even seek to take a position on – a concept that sat outside normal regulations and could potentially damage its existing currency business? We saw the opportunity to rethink this. We wanted to look beyond what cryptocurrencies have come to represent and at what they really are, how they work, what their value might be, and the potential to use them in a way that is more transparent and more aligned with regulated currencies.

WHAT DOES CRYPTOCURRENCY MEAN FOR A BANK?

With this premise, we put a group together to review potential uses for cryptocurrencies, what customer group we should focus on, and what role the Bank might play. We directed our efforts towards how we could use cryptocurrency among our institutional clients. Whether we could use cryptocurrencies as a new asset class or as a means of conducting cross-border transactions.

The problem was that while we could think about cryptocurrencies conceptually, we lacked the foundational understanding of how they operated, who was using them and why. So, we took a team of 20 people to a leading cryptocurrency business in Hong Kong, which was an eye-opening experience. Traditionally, you expect legal and compliance teams to greet new ideas with a 'No', which can feel like a brake on the business. Engaging them up-front in the fact-finding and evaluation stage was useful to identify potential challenges and find ways to overcome them.

During this visit, we pinpointed the value proposition for Standard Chartered in cryptocurrencies. Cryptocurrencies could become an entirely legitimate and potentially exciting mainstream asset class and a way to hold value, as well as a means to conduct transactions. The problem for many institutions, and a bank, in particular, is that cryptocurrencies are unregulated. However, we recognised that this objection would be less significant if we could create a 'crypto-custody' service that resembled, and created the same assurances as, a custody service for traditional assets. A bank would be an ideal partner based on its existing experience, enabling clients to explore the legitimate – and potentially very positive – potential for cryptocurrencies without the tarnish of negative headlines.

At that time, in late 2018, the Bank had several other priorities, and cryptocurrencies were less interesting than initiatives closer to the core business. However, it also coincided with the formation of SC Ventures, which allows us far greater freedom and opportunity to develop the proposition further. In December 2018, we were approached by a trading house in the UK that had learnt we were exploring crypto-opportunities and expressed an interest in partnership with us.

We continued to refine the business model, technology and product offering for a new crypto-custody service before and after the launch to the market. The service offers institutional clients, including fund and asset managers, the ability to present a new asset class to investors, but with the assurance of a bank custodian.

LOOKING BEYOND CONVENTIONAL WISDOM

We have learned much from the journey towards the launch of the new business. When we started, our experience of and attitude towards cryptocurrencies was similar to those of the wider population – namely, zero experience. Most of us had never looked beyond the media headlines and simply accepted what is presented to us at face value. However, we believed that creating the structures of trust around cryptocurrencies that clients expect, creates the potential for truly global currencies that negate the need for foreign exchange, the concept of cross-border flows and, ultimately, the role of clearing houses.

CARRYING ON PAST 'FALSE PEAKS'

Being able to adopt a different way of thinking was important when putting together our game plan for a cryptocurrency project. In most projects, you ask lots of questions up-front and define the criteria for success. You then take the starting point and identify the endpoint and create the steps to reach it. Then you measure the progress of these steps.

For this type of project, there is no fixed endpoint, so it is difficult to know what steps will take you there. This can be both liberating and frustrating. When we reflect, we can see ways to complete a project quicker and more efficiently. This can also be demoralising at times. It is a bit like trekking a mountain range. You see a peak ahead of you and put all your efforts into reaching it. Then you find that it was not the real peak at all; you need to go down and then back up again, as there is yet another peak ahead. And yet, without those 'false peaks', without embracing uncertainty and trial-and-error along the way – whether in the choice of technology, project planning, use of resources or operating models – innovation projects would not usually happen at all.

COALESCING AROUND A VISIONARY MINDSET

How people engage with a project like this, and how easily they can look beyond existing prejudices was a key lesson. In some cases, people hide behind entrenched policies and procedures, fearful that moving outside of these will create blame and criticism. In other cases – and often where you do not expect it, particularly in those whose job it is to identify and manage risk, such as Legal and Compliance – people can quickly see the vision and lend their skills and expertise to achieving it. Inevitably, every project needs a diverse team; but finding support can significantly speed up success and turn innovative ideas into viable businesses.

TAKEAWAYS

- You have to look beyond the headlines to take opportunities with new technologies.
- Go to the source to gather your information and learn from their experience.
- Support for projects can come from surprising places so keep an open mind.

24

COMPLIANCE: THE AGILE COMPLIANCE OFFICER

Benedicte Nolens

Previous Member, Compliance Lead

"Change requires agile action and decision-making."

MAKING THE JUMP

In early 2019, I received a call from Simran Gill at SC Ventures: they had done their research and thought my profile might be a match for leading the SC Ventures Compliance workstream. At the time, I was at Circle, working for the CEO and having a ball in the emerging field of crypto assets. So, I had doubts about leaving for a new role.

As the first New York Department of Financial Services Bit license holder, there were many rules applicable to Circle. We had a strong and vibrant compliance team and took a more phased and risk-prioritised approach, just as any startup would. Financial institutions used to do this when they were smaller, including when I helped build up the compliance framework for the Asian footprint of Goldman Sachs 24 years earlier. For me, this was the greatest difference about life at Circle – it was free – free to think, free to be agile, free to innovate.

Two months later, my future boss sent me a message assuring me that, if what was holding me back was the worry that I would not have enough to do, this certainly would not be the case at SC Ventures. That convinced me to make the leap – and indeed, from the day of my arrival, I have not stood still. In only two years, we had laid the foundations for the ventures you are reading about in this book. Each of them has required different, right-sized compliance approval and focus, and the paragraphs below detail my learnings and recommendations.

Change – particularly as it relates to innovation and fintech – requires agile action and decision making. The Senior Manager & Certification Regime (SMCR), introduced after the 2007 Global Financial Crisis, makes both of these actions difficult. SMCR brought a level of demonstrable personal accountability to roles, that was not there previously.

THE IMPORTANCE OF DELEGATION

For startup-style innovation to work in a bank's governance, you need to start by defining who has the authority to set the compliance programme. Unless this authority rests with the Chief Compliance Officer (CCO) of the venture arm, it will be a difficult and slow ride, as any other person will need to escalate many matters that they could otherwise have resolved. In our case, approval wait times post-escalation could take many months – too long in the context of new ventures.

To achieve proper delegation and understand our degrees of freedom (or lack of them), we needed to map out and understand the legal and regulatory obligations that applied to the corporate group and, therefore, its startup ventures. For example, the degrees of freedom of foreign subsidiaries of UK banks are confined by subsidiary undertakings under the Companies Act. So, it took us many months to get the proper definition of these obligations, but once we did it, the direction of travel became a lot clearer.

After these foundations were in place, SC Ventures needed an experienced CCO who would properly prioritise the focus between different ventures all at different stages.

We broadly did this as follows:

We determined if the venture needed a regulatory licence to operate. If so, its governance would need to closely mimic the

Bank's. If not, we had more freedom to create the right-size policies and standards. We spent a lot of time on this effort.

If regulated, we recommended hiring a venture compliance team early, as they needed to help integrate compliance systems and regulatory technology. The venture would only succeed if this was done during the design and build of the tech stack. We found this was especially relevant for the following technologies: non-face-to-face onboarding, fraud control, sanctions name screening feeds, and transaction screening.

For unregulated ventures, we gave startups more leeway while maintaining key policies and standards, either due to legal and regulatory obligations on the group or for good hygiene purposes.

We balanced agile with the disciplined phasing of compliance work across the portfolio of ventures. No day is the same when working with one startup, and even less so when working with many of them at the same time. Every day was disrupted by a multitude of issues, and it took a lot of discipline to remain focused on what had to be in place before the beta launch of every venture in the portfolio.

We supported learning by design. Startups do not have unlimited budgets and they can easily burn through cash. This meant that it was essential for the CCOs to roll up their sleeves and draft, plan and execute tasks by the timelines set.

TAKEAWAYS

- The issues of delegation and degrees of freedom in a compliance function, is largely dependent on the legal and regulatory obligations of the corporate group and its startup ventures.
- It is important to carefully manage the prioritisation of different ventures all at different stages, with different compliance requirements.
- Positive behaviours for an agile compliance officer include a willingness to help, empathy, and transparency regarding priorities and timelines.

25

LEGAL: THE T-SHAPED COUNSEL

Agnieszka Verlet

Member, Legal Lead

"A lawyer who learns how to walk the line between the traditional approach of an incumbent institution and the requirements of an agile, technology-savvy corporate startup, will propel innovation."

Working in SC Ventures is not for the faint-hearted. It is super-challenging, mostly in a good way. SC Ventures is not about 'quick wins' or digitising existing business propositions. It is about completely reimagining the business and creating new revenue streams. The job covers a whole spectrum of traditional legal expertise, from commercial to Information Technology, from payments to venture capital advice. It naturally includes emerging new areas: legal and regulatory issues relating to blockchain, digital assets, AI and data analytics.

To do it well, we needed to be a jack-of-all-legal-trades and, simultaneously, continue to develop our key legal expertise. The focus was more on real life, too. It was about the delivery, rather than about providing advice *per se*. Legal needs to work with the team closely, take responsibility for understanding the details of the whole project, follow its many turns, and be prepared to answer the question "Can we do it?" and also think about how we could do 'it' better.

Every day was different. We might need to provide strategic advice on the approach to blockchain consortia or to sign off on non-disclosure agreements with five startups. Three things were certain, though: it was never boring; days never went as planned, and there was always much more to do than time allowed.

ENABLING INNOVATION

Legal professionals have an important role to play during digital transformation. The new models cut across existing business and product lines and venture into territories the organisation had not previously explored. To help the change, lawyers need to identify key legal and commercial risks and bridge gaps between separately organised and managed teams.

Lawyers need to upskill, to gain a deep understanding of the new business models. The transformation work will look different depending on what it involves, and many variables may be unfamiliar. For example, setting up a technology platform connecting small and medium-sized enterprises with service providers requires a fundamentally different legal approach than advising on the provision of financial services. It requires stepping into the shoes of a technology-based service provider while remembering that the technology provider remains part of a regulated organisation. Striking the right balance is not easy. However, a lawyer who learns how to walk the line between the traditional approach of a regulated institution and the requirements of an agile, technology-savvy corporate startup, will propel innovation.

UNDERSTANDING THE CROSS-BORDER DIMENSION

Working in SC Ventures brought a new perspective – advice on matters that systematically carry multinational elements. As technology crosses borders easily, business models can be replicated and scaled at a much greater pace. Even when a venture is built for a single country, we needed to understand whether that business model could be replicated elsewhere. This required basic knowledge of diverse legal ecosystems in other countries, but also an understanding of how regulation changes might impact these ventures in the future. Bear in mind, though, that this means having a broad understanding to make the project building easier without creating detailed and time-consuming analyses for all potential jurisdictions.

REDEFINING THIRD-PARTY RELATIONSHIPS

Corporate governance models of third-party management are often based on the traditional dichotomy between third-party vendors supplying services to the organisation, and the organisation offering products to its clients. Relationships with service providers are managed by procurement teams who make sure that purchasing costs are within budget. Service providers are typically chosen from a range of reputable organisations. Contract templates need to accommodate enterprise-wide needs. They are complex and negotiations take months to complete. Once signed, the contracts include a variety of agreed services across the organisation and often in many locations.

This traditional approach does not work when contracting with fintech startups, which are often small, without in-house counsel and with no spare cash for external lawyers. Fintechs may not be accustomed to dealing with regulated companies and their organisational and regulatory complexities, either because they are exploring new business models themselves (through partnering with a financial institution) or because they are relatively new to the market. Their financial stability may be below what a big organisation would typically expect of its suppliers. Financial arrangements may not follow the traditional 'fee for service' model. Revenue from these relationships may be linked to the value of future transactions or to the number of referrals. Fintechs' business models may be based on offering a commoditised service that, in order to remain cheap, cannot take into account the individual requirements of its clients.

Understanding this difference between traditional, vendor-type contracting and the new ecosystem of partnerships with fintech startups and other entities, is key to protecting the organisation in the main risk areas, while not exposing these vendors to a tsunami of contractual requirements. It is essential to make risk-aware but commercially realistic judgement calls.

CHANGING OF THE GUARD

A good illustration of where the old world meets new is the approach to ownership of intellectual property. Traditionally, big organisations wish to own what has been specifically created for them. However, when it comes to understanding 'why' they would want to own intellectual property or, even more importantly, 'what' it is worth protecting, it is often less clear. Startups often improve their products, thanks to the number of clients they work with. That one improved product may be their only market offering. Without being able to improve it and provide it to multiple customers, they will not be able to scale. Without scaling, they will not attract investment. Without investment, they are more likely to fail.

It takes a good mix of commercially sensitive lawyers and forward-looking businesses to find the right balance in each case. During negotiations, intellectual property often gets everyone's heartbeat up, but finding a solution that satisfies the commercial needs of everyone involved is a skill. For this, you need a T-shaped legal 'dream team'.

THE NEED FOR THE T-SHAPED LAWYER

The term 'T-shaped professional' is often used to describe the type of person who has both in-depth knowledge in one discipline (the vertical line in the letter 'T') and broad knowledge and experience across other disciplines needed to collaborate with experts and encourage innovation (the horizontal line).

Lawyers in corporate organisations are traditionally I-shaped – they are specialised problem solvers in certain areas of the law.

Legal: The T-Shaped Counsel

As their careers progress, on their way to becoming general counsel, lawyers gradually gain further skills – mainly leadership and a variety of business skills. However, when it comes to transformative projects and new business models, all lawyers, irrespective of their seniority, need to be 'T-shaped' and have the following characteristics:

Doers and owners: Being an advisor is not enough; it is important to feel part of the team, to understand the whole business proposition, and to be willing to roll up their sleeves, lead (often, to project manage) and to take ownership for the end result.

Co-operators: Advising on complex projects requires close co-operation with other lawyers and people from across the organisation. Empathy, positive communication and other soft skills are key ingredients of effective co-operation.

Understanding technology: Of course, lawyers need to use technology to do their work efficiently. More importantly, they need to understand the evolving technology that underpins digital transformation, as well as the risks associated with it, to provide adequate contractual protections.

Transforming from within: Doing things differently requires imagination and courage. It also needs knowledge of the institution, its processes and the unwritten rules of successful engagement. That knowledge takes time to gain, and more time to understand well enough to change. With the right attitude and a mix of soft skills, lawyers can then secure the support of subject-matter experts to offer end-to-end solutions.

Being comfortable with discomfort: You may not get instructions that will give you a full picture, or the instructions may be out of date by the next day, because the project has taken a turn in a new and exciting direction. Remember, this is an experiment. Uncertainty is okay. It is all about mindset: take a step back, then take a deep breath and jump. Just be sure to keep your eyes open.

TAKEAWAYS

- New business models influence our approach to legal risk: cross border nature of ventures, dependency on ecosystem of third parties, and value of intellectual property, should be analysed case-by-case.

- Lawyers working on innovative projects need to be T-shaped: in addition to obtaining technical skills, lawyers need curiosity, competencies and soft skills that will enable effective solutions.

- Collaboration is key: the ability to make a right judgement call in an environment of imperfect information flow is increased in a collaborative environment.

26

FINANCE: CASH IS KING

John Harvie

Previous Member, Finance Lead

"The key to surviving is having a flexible model."

TOO MUCH INFORMATION CAN BE DANGEROUS

Everybody hates people who change their minds, but that is a fact of business, especially when the business model evolves from something that looks like a back-of-the-envelope calculation into a strategy for world domination. Plus, managing future estimates can be challenging – more so if the alpha and beta tests of the startup do not validate the business model. Meanwhile, the key to surviving is having a flexible model. For our ventures, this meant embedding scenario-based thinking in our modelling to help 'flex' assumptions as the world around us changed.

Writing about accounting is always going to be a challenge. But doing accounting in SC Ventures was more than that: it was an adventure. Every day, there was something new; there was stuff I had not even practised since I qualified. That was when the realisation hit me: being in the banking world was like living in a bubble. The real world was different, and bridging that divide was the challenge; it was not going to be an easy ride.

"Banking is like living in a bubble. The real world is something different. Bridging that divide is the challenge."

What was expected of the Chief Financial Officer (CFO) in such a setting? Essentially, anything with a number landed on my desk. There were profit and loss statements, balance sheets and invoices; I was helping to set up the payroll, applying for bank accounts, valuing unlisted private equity, managing Basel requirements, assessing which accounting software to use, and issuing preference shares in India. Other questions that came my way: what are the accounting requirements for crypto? Do I need a nodal account? Are escrow accounts caught by specific legislation? What is a PFLP (private fund limited partnership)? What is an ESOP (employee stock ownership plan)? Oh, and could I open a cost centre?

The outward perception might have been that it was Amateur Night at the Apollo. The reality was that we were in the business of experimentation. We were not the first to do this: every major bank had an accelerator and some a venture building arm, and several even had their own fund. But very few had all three under one roof, giving us the unique opportunity to find new tools to track, monitor and report – increasingly systematically – on each of these efforts. Along the way, there was a series of lessons, which I will explain in detail in this chapter.

AVOIDING ANALYSIS PARALYSIS

We focused on simple data in two categories: 'people' and 'things'. These included:

- **Metrics** (only those that would make a difference).
- **How much cash** we had, and how much we had spent (and, ideally on what).
- **How many people** we had, and how much they cost per month.
- **What other outgoing items** we had, and how long we were committed for.
- *The run rate and its pattern* – was it flat, or getting worse?

Finance: Cash is King

Let us be frank: most people are number blind, and most users of financial or numerical information are either uninterested or find it poorly presented. We learnt that, more often than not, the solution to this was to draw a picture. It sounds simple, but boiling down complex issues into digestible chunks is an art.

We often used the following methods:

- **The waterfall model:** Used by investor relations departments the world over, this method creates a 'bridge' between one number and another, with slices of explanations in movement.

- **Materiality:** We applied the 80:20 rule, focusing only on the numbers that made a difference.

KEEPING A CLOSE EYE ON THE BURN

(The average cost per employee) x (the number of people) offers a guide to the run rate.

Of all financial metrics, cash burn is the single most important one for a startup. Without cash, it cannot pay its bills or its staff. Accurate forecasts of the burn rate, through the use of the 'run rate', are critical to making sure that the available cash lasts. Early in the venture life cycle, people are the largest running cost: the more staff, the higher the cost. This number includes their salary, medical insurance, employer taxes, payroll processing, bonus payments, and so on. By implication, the average cost per employee, multiplied by the number of people, offered us a good guide to the run rate.

Aside from the spending on people, there was also spending on 'things', including third-party vendors and suppliers (important in a startup context). The trick was making sure to monitor that we got what we paid for. If you had work done on your house, and it was not finished, you would not pay. The same applies here.

PAPERWORK AND PROCESSES MATTER

When a venture is heading towards an alpha or beta launch, the devil is in the details. Our details were endless: How would the venture get paid, and in which currency? Where would the money go? What about Goods and Services Tax (GST)? What are the processes, and what is the risk involved?

Having all the details from the start is probably unlikely, but by the time the beta launch happens, most, if not all, of the answers to these questions should have been fleshed out, factored in and, ideally, automated. Having any kind of 'manual workaround' is fine for an alpha or even beta launch, but full-scale production must be automated otherwise the venture will not scale. And scaling requires a well-thought-out process and all the artefacts that go with it. When you log on to Amazon or your online bank account, they might look slick on the front end, but how well do they work on the back end? The litmus test we used was to consider if someone buying into your venture looked 'under the hood', what would they find? Everyone assumes their idea is great, but the reality is that most deals get passed over because potential investors see beyond the 'gloss'. And if the paperwork and processes are not articulated well in a data room, your venture is not going to go far.

> *"If the paperwork and processes aren't articulated well in a data room, your venture isn't going to go far."*

GETTING THE MODEL RIGHT

While technology might play a remarkable role in reshaping modern life, only a sustainable business model – one made to last on solid foundations and sound financial modelling – can help to achieve that.

Financial model building is an art that few can execute well. Simple models have dates: ideally in months for the first six months, then in quarters, with the outer years being no more than five years at maximum. Down the side are the 'drivers': customers that drive revenue; people and things that drive cost; and underlying metrics such as customer acquisition cost, minimum viable product build, costs to launch, and so on. Phasing these into a time frame allows a financial 'story' to be built to allow challenges. Revenues have to cover costs at some stage. Without a defined and defensible plan, any venture is, at best, a bet. Having to apply the discipline of getting the model right, gave our ventures a chance to 'pause' and sense-check the environment.

TAKEAWAYS

- Avoid analysis paralysis and only track the metrics you need.
- Keep an eye on the burn and the biggest burn for any startup will be its staff.
- Attend to paperwork and processes so that you have the answers for investors.
- Get the model right so you can sense-check what is happening.

27

AFTERWORD: BRACE YOURSELF FOR MORE CHANGE

Alex Manson

CEO, SC Ventures

Here are some thoughts I shared during a keynote address at the 2020 INSEAD Finance graduation ceremony.

Let me start by saying "Congratulations!" You have completed 18 months of a Master of Finance at INSEAD. This is hard work; in fact, it is a huge personal commitment, often involving family (who will have seen a bit less of you during that time) and applying real personal sacrifice (you have had time for work ... and not much else). The sheer fact you are completing it says a lot about who you are. Now that it is behind you, it begs the question "What is next for you?" I hope we can take a few minutes to reflect on that question.

A TIME OF CHANGE

You are graduating in Finance at a time of dramatic shifts and transformation in the industry, driven more by what is happening in the world in general than in finance itself:

- There is a societal backlash against business. The last 50 years of harmony are not the norm.

- Technological disruption is being driven by a combination of computing power and the production of massive amounts of data. (You may well experience singularity in your professional life. Think about it …)

- Conventional corporations are struggling against the rise of platforms.

THE ROLE OF FINANCE

You are graduating at a time when the role of finance is being questioned for the first time in a long while, and yet (and this is a firm conviction of mine) the industry has never been more critical to human aspirations:

- Billions of people (an estimated 1.7 billion) are not served by or excluded from the financial system.

- Half a billion small and medium-sized enterprises (SMEs) typically account for about 60 percent of their countries' Gross Domestic Product (GDP) and yet are poorly served by financial services.

- Society expects the finance industry to demonstrably create wealth and support communities.

PERSONAL IMPLICATIONS

There is no way that these two factors – the role of finance at a time of great technological and social change – will not have implications for your personal life as a Finance graduate. I think the implications are in fact quite profound and inescapable:

- In the past, if you did not thoroughly understand accounting or discounted cash flow, you were going to be in hot water pretty soon. Today, if you do not understand what technology (data/ artificial intelligence, blockchain, cloud computing) does or can do in finance, you are already in hot water in the context of most financial institutions.

Afterword: Brace Yourself for More Change   195

- You will possibly need to reinvent yourself every five years, which is very different from what my generation had to do.
- Everything you will do, will be public, traceable and quite possibly scrutinised by society under the lens of whether or not it adds value to the community – not in your financial eyes, but in the eyes of that community.

A FEW WORDS OF ADVICE

- **Do not stop learning.** And, ideally, do not stop supporting each other in your mutual learning journey – it is more important than ever.
- **Brace yourself for change and discomfort.** That you are here implies you want to drive your own change. That is great. But you also realised how smart the people around you are, and how little you actually knew compared to what your peers in the classroom knew. That is daunting, but it should be a great feeling to embrace.
- **In particular, embrace new business models.** The one thing we know about the banks or asset managers or insurance companies of tomorrow is that they will look very different from today's organisations. How? What business models will they use? How do you experiment with them? *You* go and find out.
- **Place it all in the context of a higher purpose.** Finance has no reason to exist if it is not making life better somehow – be it by creating wealth, connecting communities of merchants, or enabling businesses to grow. This is your scorecard. Anything that does not contribute to it may not be worth doing for very long.

CONCLUSION

I cannot resist closing with a finance analogy. Everyone in this class has just bought a very real-life option. The premium you paid is the combination of your fees, time and energy spent and the opportunity cost of whatever else you could have done in that time.

The payout is a fulfilling professional life in finance, or in a context where finance is relevant, which you and I know is just about everything.

In a world of fast change and a fair amount of chaos, I would say the volatility of that option is high, implying that its value is high. Only one aspect should worry you: time value. It decays. I am now over 50 and have come to realise that money, ideas and connections are not really the limiter. *Time* is the scarcest commodity, so do not squander the value of the option you have just proudly acquired.

REFERENCES

CHAPTER 1

Browne, J., Nuttall, R., & Stadlen, T. (2016). Connect: How companies succeed by engaging radically with society. Random House.

CHAPTER 3

Christensen, C. M., Allworth, J., & Dillon, K. (2012). *How will you measure your life?* Harper Collins.

Christensen, C. M. (2010). How will you measure your life. *harvard business review*, 88(7/8), 46–51.

CHAPTER 11

Yuval Noah Harari, 2011, *Sapiens — A Brief History of Humankind*, Dvir Publishing House Ltd.

Original language citation: הררי, י. נ., & יהב, א., שרר, ע. (2011). תולדות קיצור האנושות.

Yuval Noah Harari, 2015, *Homo Deus — A Brief History of Tomorrow*, Harvill Secker

Original language citation: תומוררוו אף הסתורי תה: המחר של ההיסטוריה (2015).

197

CHAPTER 16

Amy Wallace & Edwin Catmull, 2014, *Creativity, Inc.: Overcoming the Unseen Forces That Stand in the Way of True Inspiration*, Random House

CHAPTER 17

John Doerr, 2018, *Measure What Matters*, Penguin Publishing Group

Ray Dalio, 2021, *Principles for Dealing with the Changing World Order*, Avid Reader Press / Simon & Schuster

www.ingramcontent.com/pod-product-compliance
Lightning Source LLC
Jackson TN
JSHW011105220225
79519JS00004B/24